The Helplessness of God

Biblical models of leadership

Nicholas King

THE HELPLESSNESS OF GOD
Biblical models of leadership

© Copyright 2014 Nicholas King.
Original edition published in English under the title THE HELPLESSNESS OF GOD by Kevin Mayhew Ltd, Buxhall, England.

This edition published in 2020 by Fortress Press. All rights reserved. Except for brief quotations in critical articles or reviews, no part of this book may be reproduced in any manner without prior written permission from the publisher. Email copyright@augsburgfortress.org or write to Permissions, Fortress Press, PO Box 1209, Minneapolis, MN 55440-1209.

Cover image: © iStock 2020: Abstract Watercolor Background - Pastel Coral Color - Soft Texture stock photo by Marje
Cover design: Emily Drake

Print ISBN: 978-1-5064-6032-1

For Elena Carillo King, born on 25 October 2013, and for her much-loved parents and grandparents.

Contents

About the author	7
Introduction – Authority	9
Part One: The Old Testament Evidence	17
Chapter 1: God the source of all authority (and how human beings get it wrong): Genesis 1–3	21
Chapter 2: Joseph's dream of exercising authority: Genesis 37, 39–47	27
Chapter 3: Moses and authority, and his successor: Exodus 3:1–4:23/Deuteronomy 32:49-51; 34:1-12	35
Chapter 4: Very peculiar models of leadership: The Judges	47
Chapter 5: What about David and Solomon?	55
Chapter 6: The tension between institution and charism	67
Part Two: The shape of Jesus' life	75
Chapter 7: The helplessness of God in the infancy narratives	79
Chapter 8: 'Authority' in Jesus' ministry	99
Chapter 9: Power and authority in Mark's Passion narrative (the helplessness of God)	113
Chapter 10: Power and authority in John's Passion narrative	127
Chapter 11: Power and authority in the resurrection	141
Chapter 12: The Holy Spirit	157

Part Three: Leadership by listening 167
   Chapter 13: Listening in Acts 171
   Chapter 14: An exercise in mutual listening?:
     1 Corinthians 193

Afterword: Discernment 207

About the author

Nicholas King is a Jesuit priest who, after many years in South Africa, now teaches New Testament at Oxford University. He is frequently in demand all over the world to lecture on biblical subjects.

Nicholas King has recently produced a translation of the entire Bible into English; it is thought that he is the first person for more than half a century to do so on his own. His translation, published by Kevin Mayhew, was made from the Greek. His aim was to keep as close to the original as possible, even preserving the original's grammatical inaccuracies and idiomatic peculiarities. This has given his translation a freshness that many readers have welcomed. The biblical translations offered in *The Helplessness of God* are all his own, but are made especially for this book.

In addition, Nicholas has published with Kevin Mayhew *Not That Man!*, a profile of St Paul and *The Strangest Gospel*, a study of Mark's Gospel.

For details of all Nicholas King's titles visit
www.kevinmayhew.com

Introduction
Authority

The origin of this book lies in a discomfort experienced by many people regarding the way in which authority or leadership has been exercised within Christianity.[1] The author is a Catholic and a Jesuit priest, and so inevitably has been struck by the somewhat authoritarian approach of at least some people in positions of leadership within that communion; there have been episodes that have looked like bullying, and others where transparency appears to have been wanting. Some observers link this with a state of mind known as clericalism, which has something to do with a perhaps unreflective notion of the superiority of the celibate priestly state over that of lay people within the Church.[2]

Recently I led a group of students on a study-trip to the Holy Land. Some of our group commented on how many 'grumpy' priests they had encountered, and I had to admit that there was some correlation between 'grumpiness' and being smartly dressed in some kind of evidently religious uniform (thought it is important not to exaggerate this). Others have made a link between this kind of 'clericalism' and the terrible abuse of children and the alarming attempts to cover up such abuse. In a recent book, the Professor of the History of the Church at Oxford University expresses a possible link between clericalism and clerical celibacy in this way:

---

[1]. For a recent attempt at looking at some of these issues, see Jeremy Young, *The Violence of God and the War on Terror*, Darton Longman and Todd, London, 2007. The treatment is a bit over-simplified and looks through too narrow a lens, but it raises some very important questions about the link between violence and the Abrahamic faiths.

[2]. For an excellent account of this phenomenon, see George B. Wilson SJ, *Clericalism: the Death of Priesthood*, Liturgical Press, MI, 2008.

clergy were forced into a celibacy which by no means all found natural or acceptable, and which many could observe played no part in the clerical ministry of Protestants. Some of these unfortunates took out their frustrations by exercising power over vulnerable young people, given the opportunity in pastoral educational situations in which the Church authorities had little recognition of the problem, and no developed procedure to deal with it. The Counter-Reformation emphasis on the special ontological status of priesthood did not always encourage clergy to attempt proper moral reflection on their actions. It is easy for those with privileged status to come to justify what they do with reference to that privilege, especially if they think that their status has been conferred by the Holy Spirit.[3]

There is, moreover, an epidemic in the Church of bloggers of a certain cast of mind and a self-righteous tone that sounds quite unlike the gospel, but more like that of those who opposed Jesus and found him shocking. Such people appear to spend their time attacking those who emphasise a different set of priorities within Catholicism. It is the kind of thing that happens in the power-structures of large institutions, but it is uncomfortable when you meet it in the Church of Christ.

The author has recently completed a translation of the Bible in five volumes,[4] and it was perhaps inevitable that this would set him thinking about what the Bible suggests about models of leadership.

To set this issue in context, there is clearly a wider problem with authority today. For a variety of reasons, persons in authority or positions of leadership are no longer afforded the instinctive trust that they once received: police, newspapers,

---

3. Diarmaid MacCulloch, *Silence: A Christian History*, Allen Lane, London, 2013, p.207.
4. Kevin Mayhew, 2004-2013.

politicians, doctors, priests, schoolteachers, nurses, celebrities (first built up and then systematically pulled down) and members of royal families have all felt the cold in recent years. Sometimes this is because of negative publicity ('a few bad apples', as defenders of such institutions are prone to argue). Sometimes, though, it is part of the *Zeitgeist*: the 1960s is often said to have been the period that aggressively questioned authority, or to have 'started the rot'.

It is more likely, however, that authority has always had its problems, for the certain fact is that God is the only absolute. All human authority has to be seen in that context, and if it is to be exercised unproblematically, it must be exercised in the name of God (and not a god who is constructed in the likeness of human beings, created to keep order). From that it follows that all human authority has to be, like God's authority, an act of loving service, not an unrestrained tyranny. The temptation of those in authority is always to regard their authority as unquestionable, or at least unproblematic ('How can I be doing it badly when I am so sincere?'). The test for any exercise of authority is this: is it a matter of power games or a matter of loving service? Do those who are exercising authority resist or accept accountability? Or do they leap instinctively to defend their privileges against the attack of those who can be cast as 'enemies of the truth'?

Authority is the interface between God's loving power and our own weakness; all human authority – including, alas, all religious authority – permanently runs the risk of abuse. Such abuse produces a caricature of the loving face of God, as we human beings, who need authoritative guidance because of our weakness, find ourselves exercising authority on God's behalf, and all too often getting it wrong. This book aims, without singling out particular authorities for attack, to see what sort of models the Bible might offer, and whether there is a way back from disrepute for all authority today – especially perhaps ecclesial authority.

One thing we might usefully do – those of us who are members of an institutional church – is examine our own consciences, mindful that 'we are Church'. Therefore, on every occasion that we exercise power in a way that is contrary to the gospel, we are proclaiming a gospel that is not of Christ: every time I use such power or talents as I have in order to assert my status, to make a bid for power, to make others feel inferior, then the face of Christ is dangerously obscured.

The thesis of this book is a simple one: that the Bible reveals God as the only ultimate authority, and that human authorities are all necessarily relative. All human beings tend to behave oddly when authority or power are in question, and we have to learn (from God) to temper our desires for power with love, which alone can resolve our problems about authority. And what God teaches us above all is (something we find almost impossible to grasp) that God is helpless until we make our choice, and cannot force us to choose our own good. This was powerfully expressed in a recent lecture by Timothy Radcliffe OP,[5] who understands God's self-revelation as an unceasing conversation. This means that a 'monarchic' model of authority in the Church (which may have been necessary when the Church had to assert itself over against emperors and against totalitarian states) is now being replaced by a 'conversational' or 'dialogue' model of the exercise of authority in the Jesus movement.

---

5. The Lattey Lecture, Cambridge, December 2013, as yet unpublished.

INTRODUCTION

In addition, there has evidently been a sea change in the Catholic Church since this book started to write itself, namely that a Pope has been elected who seems to be encouraging the institutional Church to exercise its leadership in a different way, a way that is closer to what the Gospels depict. More than that, Pope Francis was trained as a Jesuit. That means that at least twice in his life he will have gone through the full experience of the Ignatian Spiritual Exercises, carried out in silence over 30 days, and will have renewed that thoroughly biblical experience with his annual eight-day retreat. It seems therefore that it might be useful in this book to offer some reflections on this experience as the background from which our new Bishop of Rome has emerged.

The shape of the Spiritual Exercises is a simple one: they begin with a common-sense exercise known as the First Principle and Foundation, in which the retreatant is reminded that they are created for the praise and service of God and therefore need to make their lifestyle choices in accordance with that primary end. This leads into the first 'week' of the Exercises, in which we are brought face to face with the reality of sin. The second 'week' is given over to praying through Jesus' life and ministry. In the course of that week the retreatant is encouraged to make a decision about their ultimate way of life. In the third and fourth weeks, given over to the Passion and resurrection respectively, the decision is given what is sometimes called a 'reality check': the retreatant, faced with the consequences of Christ's choice in the Passion, comes to a point at which they must consider whether they are serious about their decision. The fourth week, in which the retreatant prays to share Christ's resurrection joy, acts as a confirmation of the decision. We shall say more at a later stage about the second, third and fourth weeks of the Exercises. At this point, I should simply like to suggest that reading the Old Testament for models of authority can, if it is handled well, function as something of a 'first week' and offer an encounter with our sinful reality.

I am not trying to suggest that all who read this book should become Jesuits, nor that they should all undergo the Spiritual Exercises; I simply want to argue that the Exercises and the text of the Bible, on which they are based, point to a way of being Church that might be of our time, subordinating our choices to what God is asking of us.

A word on the title, which speaks, alarmingly to some readers, no doubt, of God's 'helplessness'. Thomas Aquinas – that great gift to the Church from the Dominican Order – pointed out long ago that language about God is rather tricky to handle.[6] So while it may seem odd to call God 'helpless', it points to the important truth that God is, at least in some sense, left utterly dependent on our free human response. Those readers who are parents, or have watched parents performing their awesome, and profoundly respectful, task of bringing up children, will know what I mean by 'helplessness'. It would be quite simple, for example, for parents to use their superior physical power to achieve the end they desire. For the most part, however, they do not do that, and indeed, we should generally suppose that they had done some rather wrong if they were to exercise brute force in this way.

When parents get it right, they voluntarily abstain from exercising their power, and they do so out of love. Very often, in consequence, they feel utterly helpless: how do I persuade this baby to stop crying? By what means am I to entice this

---

6. *Summa Theologiae, Pars Prima*, 13:2-3. I am grateful for the help here of Fr Simon Gaine OP and Fr Gerard J. Hughes SJ.

adolescent to rejoin the human race? The helplessness is voluntarily taken on by parents out of love, for love asks for a free, not a compelled, response from the beloved. It is in that sense that this book sees God as 'helpless': because of God's love for his creatures, and God's desire for our responsible autonomy, out of love God renounces the exercise of power and remains voluntarily helpless, to see what we shall do. God never forces us, although frequently 'nudges' us, to move in the right direction.

It may be helpful to say that all translations of the biblical text are the author's own; you are advised, however, to have a Bible open in front of you, just to check that they are correct, or at any rate not wildly inaccurate.

PART ONE

The Old Testament Evidence

Introduction

In this first part, we shall look at some of the many Old Testament texts that deal with the appropriate exercise of authority, including God's authority. We shall see that when human beings get their grubby hands on power they tend to come over all funny and get it wrong. So this part of the book corresponds roughly to the first week of the Exercises, where the retreatant is invited to come face to face with God's generous love, and so find himself or herself challenged for their lack of love, and invited to acknowledge the extent to which sin has had control of their lives. The retreatant ends up gazing at Christ on the cross and asking, 'What have I done for Christ? What am I doing for Christ? What ought I to do for Christ?' That should be the effect of reading the texts that we shall be considering in this part.

CHAPTER ONE

God the source of all authority (and how human beings get it wrong)
Genesis 1–3

Those who put our Bible together showed great good sense in placing right at the beginning two (rather different) chapters about God's creation of the universe, and following these immediately with a third chapter showing how human beings tend to get God's creation wrong, with catastrophic results. It follows from this observation, of course, that all human authority must be responsive to God, and that we are supposed to treat creation in accordance with the 'maker's handbook'. If it fails in that exercise of humility, then all human authority necessarily tends towards abuse. What we have to do above all is to remember that God is, in the all-important first words of the Bible 'in the beginning' (this is just a single word in Hebrew). God is therefore absolute in a way in which nothing created can possibly be absolute.

Genesis 1:1–2:4 – God's mighty word

The author of the text looks at the whole of what we can observe – what nowadays we call 'the universe' and what they call 'the heavens and the earth' – and makes the claim that God is responsible for them; there is no authority or power that can possibly compete with that one. Then come two important stages, both described as 'separation' – between light and darkness (1:4) and between the two different kinds of water, above and below the dome of the sky (1:6-7). God does it effortlessly, so that the universe is no longer 'formless waste', or (in Hebrew, splendidly) *tohu wa bohu*. All this covers the first two 'days' of creation. Quite clearly we are not supposed to worry about these 'days' as chronological indicators; something much more important is going on here. God's authority is absolute but, as we are about to learn, the authority is exercised in the service of humanity.

What happens next is the important refrain that the poet inserts after each of the five subsequent 'days', contemplating God reviewing his own work: 'and God saw that it was good' (verses 10, 12, 18, 21, 25). The process of creation then reaches its climax on the sixth 'day' when, contemplating absolutely all of his creation, 'God saw that it was *very* good' (verse 31). The climax is the creation of humanity, formed in God's image and likeness and as 'male and female', with authority over the whole of the rest of creation (verse 28). It follows from this that all human authority is subordinated to God; and we also learn that humanity, divided into male and female, is equal in the sight of God (verse 27).

Genesis 2:4-25 – The creation of men and women

The second chapter in our portion starts, rather than finishing as in the previous section, with the creation of humanity. The human being is made out of clay, and God (who in this chapter is known by the sacred name of YHWH) breathes into the human's nostrils to give it life and make it into a 'living being'. The human is known here as 'adam', and the Hebrew word that is translated as 'clay' is 'adamah', so there is a conscious pun, and a very close relationship between the human person and the mud from which 'he' has been made (as we shall see, 'she' has not yet been created in this version). God has given this human person a beautiful world in which to walk; the creative act at this point is charmingly described as 'and YHWH God planted a garden in Eden in the East' (2:8). 'The man' is put in this garden (verse 15) to cultivate it and look after it, so it is clear who is in charge. Then he is given permission (verses 16, 17) to 'eat from any of the trees of the garden; and from the tree of knowledge of good and evil you are not to eat. On the day that you eat it, you shall certainly die'. The reader knows, of course, what is going to happen – such is God's authority, and such is our awareness of human weakness. However, the same reader may also reflect that, since representatives of the human race are still around to hear these sentences being read out, God did not impose the threatened punishment. The God of the book of Genesis (despite his undeserved reputation) is in fact a God of mercy (or helplessness), and one of the lessons that we have to learn is that any authority that human beings exercise must be administered with God's mercy.

To drive this lesson home, see God's tender concern to find 'the man' an appropriate companion (verses 18, 20). The Hebrew phrase here probably means something like 'a helper who corresponds to him/is his equal'. The divine generosity extends also to allowing 'the man' to name all the animals and birds, even if none of them turns out to be an appropriate companion. The most remarkable phenomenon here, and one that *men* will do well to remember, is that it is the 'woman' who is the highest point of God's creation, addressed lovingly by 'the man' as 'bone of my bone, flesh of my flesh' (verse 22). This passage concludes with a brief indication that marriage and sex are within the divine plan (verse 24), and that nakedness is all right (verse 25).

Genesis 3:1-24 – How things can go wrong

However, it does not work out quite as God apparently intended, with human beings regarding each other as equal and as God's gift to us. In chapter 3 we are invited to see a model of how human beings can fall into regarding themselves as gods, endowed with divine authority. It is very important indeed to read this story, not as a history of what happened long ago, but as our story and the story of our institutions. They are all, without exception, subject to the authority of God, and they all, without exception, suffer the temptation of regarding themselves as divine. The story narrated is that of how first the woman and then the man came to eat of the fruit of the tree of the knowledge of good and evil, so that in fact they gained knowledge but lost something very important; they discovered that they were naked, and (absurdly) were ashamed of the fact, and so they sewed fig leaves together. What they have done is abuse their authority, and like many other institutions since then, they have paid the price of the abuse.

There is a very telling moment in the narrative, when 'they heard the sound of YHWH God walking in the garden in the breeze of the day; and the man hid himself (and so did his wife) from the face of YHWH God, in the middle of the tree[s] of the garden' (3:8). That act of hiding themselves tells us more than anything else could about what is going on. Many institutions have responded in exactly the same way to the revelation of abuse of authority and to the discovery of 'nakedness'. And we notice what happens next – the familiar process of shifting the blame: first, the man blames the woman. Then he blames God, as he points out to the Almighty that it was 'the woman whom *you* gave me at my side'. The third act of shifting the blame is by the woman, who puts it all on the serpent. Then the serpent, having no PR spokesman, picks up the bill. That is what regularly happens when we abuse our authority; as always, it is God who has to sort out the mess. In this case, God makes leather garments for them (verse 21) to cover up their newly revealed nakedness; and it is God who has to remove humanity from the dangers that threaten if you know too much and cannot handle it.

To those who are inclined to argue that this is typical church-speak – trying to prevent people from finding things out and therefore fundamentally opposed to the scientific project – it is worth pointing out that the Church has always supported and encouraged scientific investigation, while also signalling the risk of people having expensive toys when they lack the maturity to use them properly. The splitting of the atom in 1945 is a good example of the human race equipping itself with a dangerous tool that it was simply too immature to handle.

There is, however, another point that needs to be made here, namely what we are calling in this book the 'helplessness of God'. By this I mean no more than that out of love God leaves human beings free to accept or reject the divine project; God never forces us to do so, even though responding to the project will certainly lead to our greatest happiness.

Some questions for reflection
- Do the first three chapters of the Bible offer any useful models for the satisfactory exercise of leadership in God's people?
- Is there anything in Genesis 1–3 that might give grounds for postulating the 'helplessness of God'?

- Does anything in these chapters help towards an examination of conscience on the part of you as an individual or on the part of the Church as a whole?

CHAPTER TWO

Joseph's dream of exercising authority
Genesis 37, 39–47

The drama of Joseph

The desire to be God is deep within us, doubtless because of our awareness of being created in God's image and likeness (Genesis 1:26), but when this desire makes us aim for domination, things always go wrong. Consider the splendid 'novella' that is the drama of Joseph, towards the end of the first book of the Bible. It is the most extraordinary story and depicts the working out of human desires for power (or 'authority') while reminding us who is really in charge, namely God.

Things start to go wrong at the very beginning of the narrative; Joseph is just 17, and his task is to help his brothers, 'the sons of his father's wives, Bilhah and Zilpah'. At this point it may be helpful to recall that Joseph and Benjamin were the sons not of either of these mothers but of Rachel, Jacob's favourite wife, a further portent that trouble lies ahead. Then we hear that 'Joseph brought bad reports of them to their father' (37:2), which confirms our diagnosis. We reflect, too, that it is a very bad sign that 'Israel loved Joseph better than all his sons', and that he 'made him a tunic down to his feet' to indicate that he was the favourite son. Not surprisingly, therefore, his brothers 'were unable to speak peace to him' (verses 3, 4).

So Jacob/Israel is abusing his authority as a father, and Joseph is playing the younger brother's game of trying to win that authority over to his side. The existing tension is made worse by Joseph's two dreams (verses 5-11) about his superiority to his brothers, and even his parents, which he is tactless enough to report to them. The narrator tells us that his brothers were 'jealous', while the father 'kept the matter', which presumably means that he was thinking about it (verse 11).[7] As it turns out, the thinking was not all that successful, since it resulted in Jacob sending Joseph to find out whether all was well with his brothers. Given the nature of the family crisis, we may hazard a guess that this is going to end in murder. Incidentally, it is worth noticing that Joseph, in response to his father's command, rashly says *hineni,* or 'Here I am' (verse 13); as we are going to see later, this generous reply nearly always leads to some discomfort in the Hebrew Bible.

And so it proves (verses 18, 19), although the murder attempt is unsuccessful, thanks to the interventions of Reuben (verse 21) and Judah (verse 26). As a result, Joseph is put into a well (verses 21-24). Then, at the suggestion of Judah, the decision is taken to sell him to Ishmaelites (verses 25-28). We are still in the region of power games, here, of course. Next, while all these plans are being cooked up, some Midianites lift Joseph out of the pit and sell him as a slave for 20 pieces of silver (verse 28). In consequence, as is so often the case in power games, his brothers organise a cover-up (verses 31-35) and lie to their father, who now thinks that Joseph is dead. At this point, the narrative takes a break to consider the odd story of Judah and Tamar (chapter 38), which could also be seen as a power game, but you will have to read that story for yourself.

On arrival in Egypt (39:1), Joseph becomes a slave of Potiphar, where his abilities see him rapidly promoted. Then,

---

7. See Luke 2:19, 51 for a similar idea, about Mary.

however, another power game takes place because Mrs Potiphar wishes to have sexual intercourse with this good-looking and competent slave. The reader knows the truth, and is convinced that something good will result from this, but for the moment this lady's abuse of her authority, her lust and her lies, land Joseph in prison. In prison, Joseph's talents see him promoted (verses 20-23), and he then exercises his oneirophantic[8] skills on the dreams of two of his fellow prisoners. Before doing so, however, he makes an important remark (important, that is, to the advance of the narrative): 'Surely interpretations come from God. Please recount them to me' (40:8). So the dreams are related and effortlessly interpreted (death for the chief baker; promotion for the chief cupbearer). Joseph, however, continues to languish in gaol because the chief cupbearer, who benefited from the interpretation of his dream, has forgotten all about him, until two years later when the Pharaoh himself has two dreams.

At that point (41:9-13), the cupbearer is reminded of his own dream experience and tells the Pharaoh about Joseph, who is then summoned and effortlessly (once more) tells Pharaoh what his dreams mean. For the purposes of our enquiry, we need to notice that Pharaoh's absolute authority is now relativised because the dreams are outside of his power. It is therefore Joseph's task to put before him the underlying theme of the story – that God is in charge. This makes all human authority secondary and derivative: 'Joseph answered Pharaoh, saying, "It is not I, but God, who will give an answer of peace for Pharaoh"' (41:16), and 'God has told Pharaoh what he is doing' (verse 25, cf. verse 28). All authority belongs to God, and humans are given insight, but they are not encouraged to use it for their own purposes.

---

8. This strange word refers to the ability to interpret dreams.

Nevertheless, Joseph finds himself promoted, and he turns out to be the man with the right sort of ability and integrity to sort out the food situation. Again and again it is emphasised that God is in charge (41:32), and that the person who will sort it out has to be 'a person on whom is the Spirit of God' (41:38); Pharaoh actually tells Joseph that 'God has made all this known to you; no one is as wise and perceptive as you are' (verse 39). Then we watch in admiration as Joseph sorts out the supply problems with competence and integrity. Even the names of Joseph's two sons reflect what God has done for him (verses 51-2), and because of that, all is well. Chapter 41 ends with the whole world flooding to Joseph: 'the whole world came to Egypt, to Joseph, to buy grain' (41:57).

That, of course, generates the next turn in the narrative. In chapter 42, Jacob sends his sons down to Egypt because grain is available there. This is thanks to his son's administrative brilliance, though we are the only ones who know this at present. They all go to Egypt except Benjamin, who is full brother to Joseph. The narrator employs the device of having Joseph himself distribute the rations, and he recognises his brothers immediately. He plays a power game of his own, however, and accuses them of being spies (verse 9), and when they tell him of the two brothers who are not present, he demands to see Benjamin. The brothers are locked up in prison (verse 17), then Simeon is kept as a hostage (verse 24). In the meantime the narrator gives us an important clue that all will be well, for he tells us of Joseph 'weeping' because he understands their conversation; importantly, that conversation is a frank confession of the wrong they did to him, and Reuben is given the chance to boast of his attempt to save Joseph's life (verse 22).

Joseph's tears tell us that all will be well, even after he has given orders to have the grain placed in their sacks, and the money along with it. The brothers' reaction to the discovery of what Joseph has done, though they do not realise it was he, fills them with fear and causes them to ask (and we have already seen that this is an excellent question), 'What is this that God has done to us?' (verse 28). For quite a while they have no idea what to do – or rather their father Jacob has no idea what to do. They are outside their competence and unable to manage events, and Jacob is understandably reluctant to let Benjamin go, since Simeon is a hostage and Joseph, as far as Jacob is aware, is dead. Eventually, however, the old man is persuaded by Reuben (42:37) and Judah (43:8-10). Reluctantly Jacob agrees, and insists on sending all the right sort of presents and bribes, and he also insists on returning double the amount of money that had been found in their bags.

When the brothers reach Egypt, they meet Joseph, who is ahead of the game and gives orders for a feast to be served. He brushes aside their reports of the money they have found in their bags: once again the all-important theme of divine activity is played as he tells them, 'Your God and the God of your father has given you treasures in your bags' (43:23). Next comes the formal encounter, the preliminary to the banquet to which he has invited them, and the ritual enquiry after their father. This is followed by the enormously touching moment when for the first time Joseph sees Benjamin, whom they have brought with them. He is so overcome with emotion that he has to leave the room.

All seems to be well now, but the power games are not over, for Joseph has another trick up his sleeve. At first it sounds generous, for the money they have paid is to be returned to them. Then, however, we overhear Joseph giving instructions to 'put my silver cup into the youngest one's bag' (44:2), and he will subsequently use that as a pretext for enslaving Benjamin. The brothers are taken back to Joseph, who continues playing his power game: 'What is this deed that you have done? Didn't you realise that a man like me does divination?' (44:15). They have no power games left to play and, slightly surprisingly, admit their guilt, 'God has found out the guilt of your servants; look – we are slaves of my Lord' (verse 16). Pleasingly, Judah plays the solidarity card; in a very moving speech he tells the unvarnished truth (44:18-34). He insists that it is all for one and explains the situation with regard to their father – that it will kill him if they go back without Benjamin (44:30, 34). That is enough, and the narrator takes us to the dramatic moment that we have been longing for, when the Egyptian potentate reveals himself as Joseph.

Joseph interprets the situation to them (and to us, of course), and three times says that 'God sent me here ahead of you' (45: 5, 7, 8); it has always been God who has been in charge. This is the underlying theme of this story: although they have all behaved badly, it has nevertheless been God's work all the time. That is one of the rules of the biblical narrative – that God is in charge, and will bring his project to completion in spite of human sinfulness and power games. The brothers are sent on their way with a final, significant instruction that there are to be no recriminations on the way (45:24).

Now the story is (as far as we are concerned) almost over, as the brothers go back to get their father Jacob. However, one important event remains, when Jacob sacrifices at Beer-Sheba and God appears to him to give him the courage to go down into Egypt: 'Jacob, Jacob . . . I am the God, the God of your father. Don't be afraid to go down into Egypt' (46:1-3). All is well, and in chapter 47 Pharaoh shows old-fashioned oriental courtesy to Joseph's family and tells them to take what land they want. It is a happy ending, for sure, but the alert reader will notice that none of the power games have made it so, but only the unfailing action of God, which is what this highly entertaining story is really all about.

Some questions for reflection
- Who in the Joseph story is without blame?
- Does anything in the narrative apply to the situation of Christian churches/the Catholic Church today?
- Does this story enable us in any sense to speak of the 'helplessness of God'?

CHAPTER THREE

Moses and authority, and his successor
Exodus 3:1–4:23/Deuteronomy 32:49-51; 34:1-12

1. The authority of Moses

The next episode to look at is the first sketch of the question of authority within the people of God, and the first carrier of the office (who had, it must be said, a very rough time of it) was Moses. 'Of course', you say, thinking that every schoolboy knows that Moses was the leader of the people of Israel, but we need to remember that at the time of the encounter with God that gave him his authority, he was a) Egyptian; b) a murderer on the run; c) a shepherd married to a Midianite lady, for no better reason than that he had been nice to her at a well. This is not a very promising candidate for leadership of the people of God, but that is God's decision, not ours. And we should notice the way in which the narrator introduces the story:

> The children of Israel groaned because of their slavery, and they called for help, and their cry for help went up to God, from their slavery.
>
> *Exodus 2:23b, 24*

So we know, before we have even heard of Moses' vocation to exercise authority, that the calling comes from God, and that his mission is to help liberate the oppressed. God is in the narrative, and that is what makes the difference. Then the story takes on a very serious tone: we are on Horeb, 'the mountain of God' (3:1), and Moses is just going about his ordinary business when he finds himself puzzled by the burning bush,[9] and the puzzle leads him deeper into a mystery that is none of his making. The reader notices how God is involved at every level of the story, from the cry going up from the oppressed, through the 'angel of God flaming out of a bush' (3:2), to the identification as both 'Lord' and 'God' (3:4). Then comes the telling moment, which we should set against every supposed summons to exercise God's authority, for our runaway murderer is addressed twice –'Moses! Moses!' Moses is unwise enough to respond *hineni*, or 'Here I am,' which, as we have said, is a sure-fire recipe for trouble.

Next the reader is given a further reminder that Moses is not in charge: 'Do not approach. Take the sandals off your feet; the place on which you are standing is holy ground' (3:5). This insistence on holiness and on the presence of God in the narrative provides us with the context in which Moses is to exercise his authority, and the context in which all human beings are invited by God to exercise authority. Instead of tying on our hobnailed boots, we are to tread very gently indeed, and to remember always the overriding claims of the holiness of God.

Then God identifies himself: 'I am the God of your father, the God of Abraham, the God of Isaac, and the God of Jacob.' Moses shows that he is fully aware of the nature of the game that is being played, as the narrator tells us that 'Moses hid his face, because he was afraid to look upon God' (3:6). Once again, he is (and we are) reminded that the task that Moses is being given is not something that he has chosen but rather is something that is placed upon him; nor is it a task given to him to increase his status or improve his financial situation. God tells him:

---

9. 'Why is the bush not burned?' he exclaims in 3:3.

> I have certainly seen the affliction of my people who are in Egypt, and I have heard their outcry because of their taskmasters, for I know their sufferings. And I have come down to rescue them from the power of Egypt . . . so now come, and I am going to send you to Pharaoh, and you are to free my people, the children of Israel, from Egypt.
>
> *Exodus 3:7-10*

At this interesting juncture, Moses points out his own inadequacy for the task: 'Who am I that I should go to Pharaoh and deliver the children of Israel from Egypt?' (3:11). The only answer he receives (verse 12) is, 'I shall be with you,' and a sign whose fulfilment lies some way in the future – 'that you will all worship God on this mountain'. Moses is not entirely at ease, however, and asks a perfectly sensible question, which you might translate as 'Excuse me, but who am I talking to?' God does not seem to object to this line of enquiry, and tells Moses that he can tell the Israelites that his name is 'I Am Who I Am' (and we have to admit that there are several ways of translating this Hebrew expression[10]). God then continues:

> This is what you are to say to the children of Israel: YHWH the God of your ancestors, the God of Abraham, the God of Isaac, the God of Jacob, has sent me to you: this is my name for ever, and this is my title for all generations.
>
> *Exodus 3:15*

Now, however, Moses is faced with the tricky bit. First he has to summon 'the elders of Israel' and persuade them that their God has sent him (verse 16). We need to recall at this point that he is, as far as they are concerned, an Egyptian, and therefore not likely to have credibility among his fellow

---

10. Ehyeh-asher-Ehyeh, or אֶהְיֶה אֲשֶׁר אֶהְיֶה if you want to know what it sounds and looks like in Hebrew.

Israelites. Secondly, he and the elders are to go to the King of Egypt and jointly give that somewhat tyrannical monarch a message from God to the effect that 'YHWH, the God of the Hebrews, has appeared to us; and now, please, let us go on a three-day journey into the desert to sacrifice to YHWH our God'. And, not surprisingly, God warns Moses that the King of Egypt will not let Israel go, 'no – not even by a mighty hand' (though the text is a bit uncertain here).

So this invitation to exercise authority is not especially attractive, and Moses, frankly, demands evidence. God therefore does various interesting, not to say alarming, things with Moses' staff, as well as briefly inflicting on him a touch of leprosy (4:1-9).

Next Moses takes another tack – that he is worried about his lack of eloquence, so God agrees[11] that his brother Aaron will do the talking while Moses will perform the signs (4:10-17). At that point, Moses has no further objections and asks for his father-in-law's permission to go back to Egypt, which is granted readily enough. And we see that, with Aaron's assistance (4:27-31), Moses gains in authority.

This is the beginning of the mission, and it is not going to be easy for Moses. As God predicted, the Pharaoh plays a very difficult game – in the end only conceding when forced to do so – and acts the part of a hard-nosed and adroit politician from beginning to end. For a flavour of the negotiations that go on, you might read reflectively through Exodus 5:1–15:21.

Pharaoh is a difficult negotiator, and Moses' people don't show much in the way of gratitude, either. Those who have exercised authority among the people of God may feel some sympathy for him, of course. The complaints start in 5:19-23,

---

11. Not without some divine irritation – see 4:14.

when Moses is accused of causing trouble with their oppressors, and Moses in turn complains to God (5:22): 'Lord, why have you treated this people badly? Why did you give me this mission?'

Surprisingly enough, the complaints start in earnest once the Israelites have left the land of oppression, when God and Moses have brought them the liberation they have been praying for. Inevitably Pharaoh changes his mind and sends his crack troops after Israel, and the Israelites blame Moses (14:11, 12) in strikingly harsh terms:

> Was it because there were no graves in Egypt that you took us to die in the desert? What is this that you have done to us in taking us out of Egypt? Isn't this just what we told you, in Egypt, when we said, 'Leave us alone, and we'll be slaves to Egypt? For it is good for us to be slaves to Egypt – better than dying in the desert?'

The complaints go on: in Exodus 16:2, 3 we discover that 'the whole congregation of Israel grumbled against Moses and Aaron' – God's representatives (the word translated as 'congregation' has a certain solemnity to it); but God's generous response is to give them manna and quails. And if you thought that would put an end to their complaining, read Numbers 11:1-6, where they complain that 'we have nothing but this manna to look at', and show their complete ingratitude for what God and Moses have done for them. Or turn to Exodus 17:3-7, where the complaint is that they have nothing to drink, and so Moses is instructed to strike the rock and produce water from it. He does so, but is not exactly overwhelmed by their gratitude in response. Or look at Numbers 14, where because of the report by Caleb's companions they at first decide that they can't possibly go into the Promised Land, to which they have been journeying all this time (see Numbers 13:28, 31-3). So God loses patience and decides to wipe them all out (14:12), but Moses persuades him otherwise. As a result their punishment is reduced to not being allowed to enter the Land, and the wandering of the people is increased from 40 days to 40 years. Finally the people repent, and are all for going to the Promised Land after all, but Moses tells them that it is too late (14:39-43).

It is not only the people at large who go in for grumbling, for Aaron and Miriam (Moses' own brother and sister) complain about Moses' authority, or rather perhaps make a bid for power, as religious people are often prone to do, often from the loftiest of motives. Miriam is punished with leprosy, and Aaron pleads for her (Numbers 12:1-15). The narrator offers a terrible warning against complaining about God's chosen ones!

Why, you ask, bother with all this dissidence? It is simply that the Bible reminds us that exercising authority among the people of God is never going to be easy. It is not the case, alas, that those who have faith in God always behave unselfishly and with respect for others, and we shall do well to remind ourselves of this.

Equally, of course, it is impossible for just one person to exercise power in the people of God, so at the suggestion of his father-in-law Jethro, Moses delegates his authority (Exodus 18:13-26; cf. Numbers 11:16-30). Jethro has observed how Moses sits in judgement all day long and points out that he is attempting the impossible. Once again, we see that a single person cannot exercise authority among the people.

2. The challenge of authority

Equally, of course, the people will not always get it right. The iconic story is that terrible episode of the Golden Calf, in

Exodus 32. The situation is that Moses has been summoned up Mount Sinai. The people have made a promise to do whatever God commands them, but only Moses is permitted to get close enough to God's holiness (Exodus 19:20-4) to find out about the commandments. These start with the 'Decalogue' (20:1-18), which is immediately followed by thunder and lightning. This so terrifies the people that they retreat and insist that Moses alone talk to God: 'and they said to Moses, "You speak with us, and we shall listen; but don't let God speak with us, or we'll die"' (20:19). So, at their request, Moses is the sole mediator between God and the people of God. There follow several chapters explicitating the Ten Commandments, and they include the handing over to Moses of the stone tablets on which God has written them (24:12-17). This turns out to be a rather lengthy process – six days of preliminary waiting for Moses to receive the call, and then 'forty days and forty nights', during which time he is given the tablets (31:18), as well as very specific prescriptions for the construction of the Ark of the Covenant (25:1–31:17).

Exercising authority is no easy matter; during this lengthy period, the people over whom Moses is given charge become bored with both Moses and God, so they persuade Aaron to manufacture a golden calf so that they can have something more tangible to worship. They acclaim this contrivance with the terrible words, 'Here are your gods, O Israel, who brought you up from the land of Egypt' (32:4). Words almost fail us, if we have followed the narrative thus far: how could they possibly hold such a view, after all that they have experienced? Yet that question can be put to the people of God at any stage in history, for our story is marked by foolish infidelity.

We should pay attention, however, to God's reaction, and that of Moses, his chosen delegate. Not surprisingly, the narrator puts on God's lips the most terrible reaction. First he tells Moses that they are '*your* people' (32:7), and then he gives his verdict

> I see that this is a people stiff of neck; and now, give me a break, that my anger may blaze against them and eat them up. And I shall turn you [Moses], into a great nation.
>
> *Exodus 32:9-10*

Here we see the stuff of which those who wield authority have to be made: rather than being pleased at being singled out for greatness, Moses stands up to God and argues the toss, like Abraham did back in Genesis 18:22-33, and reminds God that they are '*your* people, whom *you* brought out of the land of Egypt' (32:11). And, to the reader's astonishment, God concedes the point: 'and the Lord repented of the evil which he said he would do to his people' (32:14). We notice that this carries the implicit admission that they are indeed 'his people'. It is not an easy job to exercise authority in the people of God.

3. The death of Moses

One of the points that we are making throughout this book is that all human authority is relative, and that God's is the only absolute authority. To put it bluntly, human beings grow old and die. At the time of writing, we have recently been lost in admiration at the courage involved in the resignation of Pope Benedict XVI, for example. At some point human leaders have to lay down their authority. The narrator(s) of the first five books of the Bible are aware of this, and duly recount Moses' awareness of his own limitations:

> I am a hundred and twenty years old today, and I can no longer walk about, to go and come in, and YHWH has said to me, 'You are not going to cross this Jordan'. YHWH your God, he is the one who will cross before you.
>
> *Deuteronomy 31:2, 3*

Then the narrator recalls the problem of succession; for there is always a problem of succession to authority, and many ways of solving the problem, all of them defective. Human beings, you see, tend to behave very oddly when power is at stake. Now the narrator makes it clear that there is a successor nominated by God: 'Joshua – he is the one who will cross over before you, just as YHWH said' (Deuteronomy 31:3). The point here is well made by the grammar of the Hebrew sentence, that in a sense Joshua is doing what God does; but at the same time Joshua (or any other religious leader) is not God.

The transfer of authority is a key issue, and it might be helpful for you to examine what ways there are of such transfer: in politics, in churches, in societies and in clubs. In this case the official line is that Joshua's succession is a done deal: because Moses got things wrong back at Meribah near Kadesh, in the wilderness of Zin, he is not to be allowed to enter the Holy Land (Numbers 27:12-14). Moses graciously accepts the sanction and simply asks God:

> May YHWH, the God of the spirits of all flesh, set a man[12] over the congregation, who will go out before them and who will go in before them and who will lead them out and lead them in, and YHWH's congregation shall not be like a sheep that has no shepherd.
>
> *Numbers 27:16, 17*

---

12. The reader will be aware, I am afraid, that this is not a culture in which women's leadership can be contemplated.

This is a charming picture, but we should notice that leadership in the congregation is the gift of God, not something to be bought and sold. So Joshua is duly appointed, and made subservient to 'the priest Eleazar', so that no one should suppose that he is a potentate in his own right (Numbers 27:19, 21).

As we have already said, all human authority comes to an end, and so it duly happens with Moses. He is told to climb Mount Nebo, just opposite Jericho, view the Promised Land and then die (Deuteronomy 32:49-52). He duly does so (34:1-7), and dies a good death (a 'good death' is an important part of exercising religious authority, and is always followed, you will have noticed, with immense interest). God shows him the entire Promised Land, and then, after the ban on his entering the land has been reiterated, the narrator simply tells us:

> and Moses, the servant of God, died there, in the land of Moab, at YHWH's command. And he buried[13] him there in the valley in the land of Moab opposite Beth-Peor; and no one knows his grave until today.

The picture, then, that the biblical narrative has painted so far is this: God is the only authority, and all human authority is relative – that is to say it comes to an end, and attention must always be paid to the question of succession. Human beings are weak, in several different respects, and if ever we give in to our standing temptation to worship power, then we shall be committing idolatry, and will pay for it.

---

13. Some versions say 'he was buried' here; this is an understandable mistake.

Some questions for reflection
- Does Moses offer a model for leadership in the people of God today? If so, in what way?
- What does the episode of the 'burning bush' (Exodus 3) say about authority among the people of God?
- Does the story of the Golden Calf (Exodus 32) reveal anything of the nature of God?

CHAPTER FOUR

Very peculiar models of leadership
The Judges

Introduction

The very odd characters who are known as the 'judges' exercise what is known as 'charismatic authority'. This can seem a very attractive idea, in contrast to the 'dead hand of institutional authority'. The judges exercise power in virtue of their decisive encounters with God, and we are inclined to applaud. The difficulty with this, however – and it is as well to be honest about it – is that charismatic authority tends to end up in chaos. That was the experience of Israel as the people of God, as we shall see in the course of this chapter.

We shall not talk about all the judges here. If this arouses in you a fear that censorship is taking place, then have a look at those who are omitted; in particular, perhaps, you might read the edifying tale of Ehud and the fat king of Moab (3:12-29), and then Shamgar (3:31), Tola (10:1, 2), and Jair of Gilead (10:3-5), about whom we should love to know a great deal more than the enigmatic and intriguing remarks that we are given. We shall also not mention Ibzan of Bethlehem, Elon of Zebulun, and Abdon of Pirathon (12:8-15).

There are, however, a few judges whom we should consider in this section because of what their stories tell us about biblical attitudes to leadership. Without spoiling the story, or being unduly tendentious, I would ask you to notice that (as so often happens in the Bible) it is the woman who gets it right. That woman is Deborah (4:1–5:31). We observe her unmistakable authority, and notice that the compiler of the narrative sees no problem in having a woman speak for God: he tells us that 'she sat beneath the palm-tree of Deborah . . . and the sons of Israel went up to her for judgement. She sent and called Barak' and instructs him to attack Mount Tabor, but he only agrees to do so, 'if you come with me, then I shall go; and if you do not come with me, I shall not go' (4:5-8). It is quite clear who is doing the leadership here. A part of this story is the subplot of the murder of Sisera by Jael (4:17-22) – something you should definitely not try at home. Notice that despite the feel of the names, Sisera is a man and Jael is a woman, who uses her guile to remove the threat; and we are clearly invited to applaud her.

Then there is the well-known story of Gideon. You could not say that his story is in every respect one for us to imitate. Practically as soon as we meet him we hear him complaining to the angel of God:

> So the Lord is with us – and why have we experienced all this? Where are all the wonders that our ancestors told us about, when they said, 'Did not YHWH bring us up from Egypt?' Now YHWH has abandoned us and given us into the hand of Midian.
>
> *Judges 6:13*

Then Gideon demands signs before he will act (6:17, 37-9), although he does destroy the altar to Baal that his father had built (6:25-32), and he has sufficient faith to allow the Lord to diminish his military reserve (7:2-7). We observe that he is successful (7:22), but the success brings danger with it, for the Israelites, emboldened by their victory, ask Gideon to set up a dynasty of monarchs over them (8:22). We are invited to applaud this step, apparently, but it is clear that we are meant to disapprove when he asks for money and commits idolatry (8:24-7). Gideon has successfully circumvented the Midianite threat, but we can already see cracks in the structure. Those cracks become clearer in the antics of his son Abimelech.[14] This one makes a bid for monarchy, but his younger brother Jotham opposes him by standing on Mount Gerizim and relating the parable of the trees (9:7-21). However Abimelech's reign comes to an unexpected end, and once again it is a woman who acts on God's behalf (9:50-5). But we should notice the human frailty that makes it almost inevitable that we seek the power that comes with a leadership position.

The next leader to come to our attention is Jephthah, whose story you will find at 11:1-40. He is illegitimate, the son of a prostitute, and is driven away by his brothers (11:2). Later, however, they want him to be their commander; he insists that they promise to give him leadership[15] in the event of YHWH giving him the victory (8-10). Once again we can see the seductions of power, but we should also notice that his brothers' earlier treatment of Jepthah implies, as he sharply reminds them when they beg him to be their ruler, that he is the least significant in his family (11:6). God does not always work through the most obvious person.

The episode for which Jephthah is best remembered, however, is his idiotic vow about what he will give to God if he defeats the Ammonites (11:30, 31) and its inevitable result (11:34-40) – the killing of his daughter. The reader should notice how understated is the account of her death in 11:39. It might be worth asking ourselves what are the

---

14. The name Abimelech, significantly enough, means 'my father is king'.
15. The Hebrew word means 'head'.

implications here for the exercise of authority among God's people today.

The last of these charismatic leaders is the rollicking figure of Samson. He is the kind of figure whom for some reason Bible readers know only vaguely, so you might wish to take the time to read through Judges 13:1–16:31. This episode reveals what an unexpected person he is to take on the leadership of God's people. His story, like that of Jesus much later (Luke 1:26-38), begins with an annunciation by an angel to a woman without a child of a baby that is coming to her, along with some quite strict instructions about his upbringing (13:3-5), and a risky encounter with the divine (13:6-22), which alarms father-to-be Manoah, but to which his wife offers a reassuringly common-sense response (13:23).

Inevitably, the child turns out to be fairly eye-catching, but not for precisely the reasons that you might have hoped. On the one hand, it is true that he can dismember passing lions (14:6), but on the other hand, he has a propensity for marrying Philistine women and then being indiscreet with them so that his secrets are revealed (14:15-18; 16:4-20). We notice that by the time we reach the second attempt by a wife to extract his secrets he has clearly learnt something, since it takes Delilah four bouts of what is unmistakably spousal nagging to obtain the truth from him (16:6-17). He is good at various measures to discomfort the Philistines, and he is a man of vengeance.[16] It is not always clear whether or not we are supposed to applaud him for these tastes. Finally he dies a heroic death, killing far more Philistines in his death than in his lifetime (16:30).

---

16. You are invited to read slowly through Judges 14:19–16:3 for a flavour of it.

Perhaps the oddest thing about the Samson story is the way it ends: 'he had judged Israel for twenty years' (16:31), and the reader is left asking, 'Well, had he?' If this is what judging is meant to be, then it is not, to be perfectly frank, terribly impressive. And yet we feel that he must have done more than that in the course of his 20 years in order to have left such a strong footprint in the memory of God's people.

Those, then, are the judges – charismatic leaders, manifestly imperfect, but nevertheless real – through whom God has been at work. There are visible dangers – of inconstancy, of taking the eye off God (particularly on the part of the men), and of thoroughly flawed motivations. A careful reading of these tales reveals that we are not to expect too much in the way of edifying or virtuous behaviour.

Hints of the future

There is, however, a bit more to the scroll of Judges than this might indicate, and the book ends with some hints of how the future lies. There is the story of Micah, and the reference to Israel's constant temptation to idolatry and worshipping that which was not the God of Israel.

As a part of this story, and apparently explaining how Micah has got things so badly wrong, the narrator remarks, 'in those days there was no king in Israel; everyone did what they thought best' (17:6). The idea recurs at 18:1 and 21:24, 25. That last remark ends the Judges scroll, and is quite clearly looking ahead to 1 Samuel and the long narrative of the monarchy, which ends with 2 Kings. That set of tales will raise many question marks about the leadership exercised by the kings of Judah and Israel. However, before that the reader has to endure the appalling story, puzzling and uncomfortable, of the Levite's concubine (chapter 19), from which no one emerges with any credit. It is perhaps the very awfulness of this story that prepares us for the emergence of the monarchy: this is the kind of thing that they get up to if there is no one who can exercise leadership in God's name. Make sure you are feeling strong when you read this story – but you must read it, as it is part of the narrative that the Bible offers us of how God's people moved towards monarchy.

Next the compilers of our biblical narrative offer us a charming tale to bring back a decent taste to our mouths. In the Hebrew Bible the book comes as one of the scrolls, in the third section of the Scriptures, but in Christian Bibles it is placed after Judges. It is the story of Ruth, who became the great-grandmother of King David. Once again it is a woman (indeed two, and perhaps even three women) who get it right, and manipulate the men into furthering God's plans. Read the book for yourself, and see what it says about biblical models of leadership and authority.

Our next character is not really a judge at all, although we read in 1 Samuel 7:6 that 'Samuel judged the children of Israel at Mizpah'. (Some versions translate this as 'began to judge', which perhaps makes more sense.) Samuel acts as a kind of transition between the older, more charismatic system of leadership exercised on the basis of personal gifts and the rather revolutionary institution of monarchy. Interestingly, the people's request for this new-fangled idea is expressed in terms of judging, for we read in 1 Samuel 8:5 that the charismatic way of exercising authority over God's people has passed its sell-by date: 'And they said to him, "Look! You have grown old, and your sons are not walking in your ways. Now put a king over us to judge us, like all the nations."' The point here is that they want the latest thing, just like everyone else, but they still express the idea of authority in terms of 'judging'.

So it seems they want something like Samuel, who (according to 7:15, 16) had spent 40 years doing the rounds of the sanctuaries of Israel, though what precisely is implied in the use of the word 'judge' is not made clear. We learn at 8:1 that he is moving towards the dynastic principle, in that 'when Samuel grew old, he appointed his sons as judges over Israel', but in the next two verses it turns out that they were not cast in the same mould: 'his sons did not walk in his ways . . . they perverted the activity of judging' (8:3). The same word is used later in 1 Samuel (24:13, 16) in a context where it has already become clear that Saul has lost the divine favour,[17] and God is invoked to judge between him and David, who at this point is as pure as the driven snow.

We are witnessing therefore a change taking place, and are brought to reflect that leadership in the people of God may perhaps never be an unchanging institution. It always changes, partly in response to human sinfulness or lust for power, and partly because change is how institutions survive.

The next institution to exercise leadership in the people of God is that of the monarchy, and in the next chapter we shall look at two major examples of this leadership – Saul's successors, David and Solomon, father and son.

This chapter has taught us that Israel is moving in the direction of institutionalisation, away from the charismatic exercise of authority represented by the rather ropey lot who are the judges. This arrangement has its dangers, but so, as we shall see, does the monarchy, which falls with the fall of Jerusalem, and which is in part responsible for that fall. The

---

17. Samuel had anointed David as Saul's successor; but we should notice that it is as a king rather than a prophet or judge.

essential criterion for exercising authority on God's behalf is to be listening to the voice of God. One can see the attraction of something a little more permanent than the improvised arrangement of the 'charismatic' judges, and understand the clamour for reform that we have detected in 1 Samuel 8:1-5, but it does not, as we shall see, solve all the problems. We have always to remember, whatever model of authority or leadership we adopt in the people of God, that our only absolute authority is God, whatever temptations we may experience in the direction of something more permanent and tangible.

Some questions for reflection
- Which of the stories about judges is illuminating for the question of authority in the people of God?
- Might any of the characters mentioned here be classed as a model leader?
- Is there any sign here of what we have been calling 'the helplessness of God'?

CHAPTER FIVE

What about David and Solomon?

So, for perhaps no very good reason, we see God's people moving in the direction of monarchy. They are expressing the desire for something a little more permanent and a little less charismatic in the way of exercising authority and, as we have seen, they mount something of a clamour for the reform of the present arrangement.[18] No human situation is ever entirely satisfactory, and therefore we are always yearning for reform. So it is not surprising that the Bible offers us two different views about kings.

Monarchy: the conservative view

The first view we may call the 'conservative' reaction, and it is the instinctive resentment of the old desert nomads against the business of settling down into stable political structures. We hear the voice of disapproval in particular as the first response to the demand for reform. At 1 Samuel 8:6-18 we are given God's reaction. Initially, God's and Samuel's reactions are the same. We are not at all surprised to read that 'the word was evil in the eyes of Samuel' (8:6). We then eavesdrop on his prayer, and hear God's response:

> YHWH said to Samuel, 'Listen to the voice of the people, in everything that they say. For it is not you that they are rejecting; it is me that they are rejecting from being king over them.'
>
> *1 Samuel 8:7*

---

18. See 1 Samuel 8:1-5.

In other words, this innovation is read as a rebellion against God; and you can easily imagine the old camel-wanderers understanding it so. Then Samuel offers a list of the ways in which monarchs will get things wrong (8:11-18): exploitation of the sons and daughters of Israel to service the very new arrangements, mass takeover of crops and vineyards;[19] there will also be 'eunuchs and slaves' (8:15). Read these verses reflectively and consider what is really going on, and share the sadness of Samuel and God when the people make their response (verse 19): 'The people refused to listen to the voice of Samuel, and said, "No – let there be a king over us."'

So the Lord instructs Samuel, 'Pay attention to their voice, and you are to king-make a king[20] over them'. Samuel's bleak response is, 'Go, each of you, to your own city.' This brief verdict speaks volumes in what the prophet does not say.

Saul is therefore duly anointed king (10:1) and accepted by the people (11:15). This occurs, we may notice, after a fairly charismatic exploit in defence of Jabesh-Gilead against the Ammonites (11:1-11). The reader never feels, however, that Saul quite has a grip on the situation, and Samuel continues to rebuke Israel for having demanded this revolutionary new institution of monarchy (12:1-17); it is in effect a betrayal of the significance of God in their history, and culminates in Samuel's calling down 'thunder and rain' (12:18). At this point, the people recognise the betrayal of their ancient tradition, so they repent and, fickle as ever, ask for Samuel's prayers: 'Pray for your servants to YHWH your God, that we may not die for having added to all our sins,

---

19. This is what the Romans would later call *latifundia* – land-grabbing large estates which have never ceased to be a source of tension in societies all over the world.
20. 'king-make a king'. This clumsy English expression is an attempt to capture the sound of the Hebrew, which concentrates the reader's attention on the idea of 'king'.

the sin of asking for a king for ourselves' (12:19). So Samuel gives them a clue about how to survive: 'Fear YHWH, and serve him in integrity, with all your heart; look at the great things that he has done for you. And if you do evil, evilly, then you and your king shall both perish' (12:24, 25).

Monarchy: the radical view

There is, however, a different, more approving view of this innovation that we call monarchy. You will find it expressed in 1 Samuel 9:14–10:1, which is the account of Saul's anointing by Samuel and concludes with Samuel saying 'Has not the Lord anointed you as prince over his inheritance?' The idea here is clearly that God supports the institution of the monarchy. In the course of this chapter we shall be looking at how the story of David and Solomon, the most eye-catching of the kings of Israel, is told. We tend to assume that David and Solomon – central as they were to the history of God's people (and, when we get to the New Testament, central also to Matthew's genealogy) – were perfect models of authority. They were, of course, nothing of the kind, as we shall see in the course of this chapter. Our contention remains that, God and Jesus apart, there is no perfect model of authority in the Bible.

Saul, we observe, is in trouble from the beginning, because he did not wait for the prophet to turn up (1 Samuel 13:13, 14); later he is in trouble because he did not do what he was told – he did not kill Agag and the best of the animals (15:9). So we hear the verdict of God: 'I repent that I made Saul king, for he has turned away from following me, and has not carried out my command'. Samuel then 'called for help to the Lord all night long' (15:11). It is clear already to the alert reader that Saul's days are numbered, even if we have to wait until chapter 28 for the episode where he consults the witch of Endor and the ghost of Samuel, and then until chapter 31 for his death. The writing (as another biblical text has it) is on the wall.

David: points in favour

So we come to Saul's successor, King David, who is almost (but not quite) emblematic of how a king should be. We meet him first when God selects him, through the agency of Samuel, on an unexpected and dangerous visit to Bethlehem. The extraordinary story of his selection is told in 1 Samuel 16:1-13. Quite clearly God is in charge of the process, which leads to the selection of the youngest and least significant of Jesse's sons as king in succession to Saul. We notice that Samuel is heavily involved in politics (despite what is often claimed, you cannot possibly keep politics and religion apart); the elders of Bethlehem are well aware of this fact and are anxious to get rid of him, but you cannot mess around with the 'seer', who is furthering God's project in the world.

Then in 16:14-23 we notice how David's harp playing soothes Saul in his dark moods; thereafter the youngster goes from strength to strength. He solves the problem of Goliath (17:32-54), and we are told, as though we needed the information, that 'the Lord was with him' (18:12; cf. 2 Samuel 8:6).

David is also a model of how to behave in war, even under provocation. For example, he will not lay a hand on the Lord's anointed (1 Samuel 24:1-22; 26:8-25; 2 Samuel 1:14-16) or on Saul's family (2 Samuel 4:8-12). We notice, with approval, that he trusts in God, and is generous to those who do not match up to the highest possible standards (1 Samuel 30:6, 7, 22-5) and to his opponents (2 Samuel 19:20-2). We are invited to applaud him as he captures Jerusalem against all the odds (2 Samuel 5:6-9), and so establishes what will be the capital of the new state that is emerging as a monarchy. The reader is captivated by the bright new world that is being established here, in the move from tribe to state, from charismatic judges to dynastic kingdom. He dances before the Lord (2 Samuel 6:14) as the Ark of God is brought into Jerusalem, and although his wife disapproves (2 Samuel 6:16, 20-3), we are clearly encouraged to applaud him. He has the bright idea, though it turns out not to be divinely inspired, of building a 'house' (a temple, in fact) for God, and when the prophet Nathan, on revisiting the issue, reveals to him that it is not after all what God has in mind, David accepts the divine rebuke (2 Samuel 7:1-28). He will, of course, have to do the same again when Nathan confronts him with the terrible story of his adultery with Bathsheba and the murder of her husband Uriah (12:1-25), and he shows appropriate humility again when he is cursed by Shimei, Saul's kinsman (2 Samuel 16:5-14), and when he commits the offence of having a census of the people (24:1-17).

On these occasions David is rebuked by his prophets – first Nathan and then Gad. This is the first sign of the important tension that the Bible depicts between those in political authority and the prophets of God. It is forbidden to exercise authority without keeping your eye on God, and when things go wrong in this respect, those who have direct contact with the presence of God have to challenge those in leadership roles. This is a tension that will surface again endlessly in the people of God, including when it emerges as the Church. Both political leaders and prophets can get things badly wrong, and human beings need constantly to be reminded that God is the only absolute authority.

That, however, is looking ahead a bit. For the moment our heart is entirely with David as he weeps for Absalom (2 Samuel 19:1-5) after that unfortunate young man has been butchered by David's nephew and general, the unscrupulous Joab. In addition, we find that he engages our sympathy because he forgives his enemies.[21]

Lastly, it is clearly in David's favour that he sings psalms (for example, 2 Samuel 22). It is not just that he is a musician and able to calm Saul's 'evil spirit' (1 Samuel 16:22, 23); it is also that he has left his imprint on all of the psalms and hence on Israel's liturgy and its identity as people of God. This is clearly of some significance. It is a reminder that the function of leadership in God's people is to build up the people, not to win an audience (in contrast, for example, to the theatrical ambitions of the Roman Emperor Nero).

David: points against

However, the verdict on David is more complex than these considerations might suggest. As we have seen, he thought that he was entitled to build the Temple (2 Samuel 7:5-17), and he is chided by the prophet Nathan for his presumption[22] and reminded who is really in charge. The house is God's house, and if David is starting a dynasty, he has to be reminded that that is God's business. The dynasty itself is not above chastisement, as it is made clear to Nathan in a message that he is to pass on to David (7:12, 14):

> For when your days are fulfilled, and you sleep with your ancestors, then I shall raise up your offspring after you, who will come out from your loins, and I shall establish his kingly

---

21. 2 Samuel 19:9-41, for example – a series of stories of reconciliation taking place in Israel after the civil war.
22. Nathan had originally been in favour of the scheme – see verse 3.

position . . . When he does wrong, I shall punish him with the cane of men, and with the chastisements of the sons of men.

2 Samuel 7:12, 14

All the time we see this profound biblical awareness that it is possible for those in positions of leadership to get above themselves, and that in consequence they need to be taken down a peg or two.

This is particularly true of David when, as we have seen, he commits adultery and murder, in the terrible story of Uriah's wife (2 Samuel 11). The account starts with the telling words, 'And it happened at the return of the year, at the time when kings go out to war, that David sent Joab and his servants with him, and all of Israel. . .' In other words, the tale starts with the clear hint that David is not doing what his leadership post would lead us to expect him to do, for he is staying at home instead of going out to war at such a time. Then, just like the worst kind of leader, he thinks of himself as a god who can have what he wants, so in verse 4 we read that, after he has seen the beautiful Bathsheba, 'he sent messengers and took her, and she came to him'. This is the conduct of a leader without accountability. The inevitable now happens: she discovers (verse 5) that she is pregnant, so, like many other leaders in the people of God, David tries to engage in a cover-up, and concocts an excuse to bring Uriah back from the front. Uriah, for all that he is a foreigner (a Hittite), obediently does what David asks, but he will not sleep with his wife when 'the Ark and Israel and Judah are living in tents, and my Lord Joab, and my Lord's servants are in the open air: am I to go home and eat and drink, and sleep with my wife?' (verse 11). The reader knows, of course, that David has slept not with his own wife but with Uriah's, when the Ark and Judah were 'living in tents'; so every word convicts David for his failure as a leader of God's people. And then the king makes it worse by having Uriah murdered. It is true that in the following chapter David is brought to very profound repentance, but the reader never forgets this betrayal of his position of authority. Human beings are not God, and we reveal our weaknesses in the way we exercise leadership.

Later, David appallingly mishandles the rape of Tamar (13:6, 7) by her half-brother Amnon. One of the dangers of people with an exalted position in society is the uncritical assumption that their children are immune to ethical demands. The narrator makes an interesting and plausible psychological point when he has Amnon actually turn against Tamar, once he has raped her (2 Samuel 13:15). Eventually Absalom takes revenge and has Amnon killed (13:28, 29), all because their father David had done nothing about it (verse 21). Their relationship never recovers, despite some cunning moves by Joab (14:1-27), and eventually Absalom makes an open bid for power (15:1-12) and David has to flee from Jerusalem (15:14-37). In the end Absalom is killed by Joab, against David's explicit orders (18:5, 9-17), and David mourns him bitterly, possibly reflecting that he should have shown more affection in his lifetime (19:1).

David emerges from these pages as a real person, whom we think we know, but one who is undoubtedly flawed. He is a useful reminder that leaders in the people of God are not themselves God. A further crime, mentioned above, is that he carries out a census of the people (2 Samuel 24:1-9). Nowadays that seems a fairly harmless sort of activity, but in the Bible it is read as the king's megalomania and presumably a move in the direction of higher taxation and greater bureaucracy, or possibly, because of the reference to 'men of war, able to draw the sword', in the direction of aggression against neighbouring states (verse 9). God is in charge, however, and the story ends with the purchase of the threshing floor of Araunah the Jebusite and the building of an altar there, which look ahead to Solomon's building of the Temple on that site.

The last thing we hear against David is that he has to be kept warm by a young virgin (1 Kings 1:1-4). (Or is this a point in favour? We are firmly told that he did not have sexual intercourse with her.) In this context David is now hardly functioning independently at all. So Nathan and Bathsheba manipulate him politically, to make sure the throne goes to Solomon rather than to Adonijah, who might be thought to have the prior claim (that, certainly, was Adonijah's view). Once again there is a power struggle for leadership in the people of God, which in the end is only resolved by Solomon's butchery of Joab and Adonijah (1 Kings 2:25, 34).

Solomon: points in favour

Solomon's reign starts, therefore, with something of a shadow over it, and the logic of the narrative suggests that all is not going to end well. However, it was in many ways a brilliant reign, and there is much to be said in Solomon's favour. For one thing, and very strikingly, when God tells him to ask for anything that he might desire, he asks for wisdom instead of wealth or long life or the killing of his enemies (1 Kings 3:5-15), and since God congratulates him on this choice, we, too, are clearly meant to applaud the young man.

Nor is that the only point in his favour. We learn, for example, that he judges wisely, and we are given the example of the appealing, though undeniably risky, solution he gave to the problem of the two prostitutes in dispute over which one's son had died (3:16-28). Then, of course, he builds the Temple (5:15–6:38); the careful description and the length allotted to it means that we are to take it very seriously indeed, and to applaud Solomon for having achieved this construction. Not only that, but once the Temple is built, he prays appropriately in the sanctuary in just the way that a good leader should (8:14-53), reminding God of the promise of a Davidic succession to the throne, and asking God to listen to the prayers that are uttered in the Temple and to forgive the sins of those who ask for pardon. Then he pronounces a priestly blessing over the people of Israel (8:56-61), with a reminder of how they are to respond to God. At this point we are clearly meant to see Solomon as a model leader for the people of God, and this impression is strengthened when God talks to him (9:1-5) and confirms that all his prayers will be heard. We should notice, though, the clear lesson that (once more) it is God who is in charge, and there is a stern warning for those in authority who might forget the precious lesson (9:6-9).

Solomon is a highly successful monarch, even in purely secular terms. His building projects are immense (9:15-23) and he has a huge team to accomplish them. He also runs a sizeable fleet – the only time in its history that Israel is a serious naval power (9:26-8). In addition to all this, he even impresses the Queen of Sheba (10:1-13), a searching examiner who gives the young king the highest possible marks. He is also phenomenally wealthy (10:14-29). There is much to be said in his favour.

Solomon: points against

All of this aggrandisement of one human being, however, will inevitably have raised questions in the minds of the readers. Has he, they will be asking themselves, lost sight of the fact that he is the servant of God's people? Certainly there is a good deal to criticise in this apparently most successful of monarchs who is, significantly enough, the last king to reign over the artificial alliance of Israel (in the North) and Judah (in the South). For one thing, he is clearly quite ruthless,[23] and it is far from clear that we are meant to applaud him for his elimination of actual or potential enemies. For another, he has a vast bureaucracy (4:1-19; 10:14-29), which is fulfilment of Samuel's warning in 1 Samuel 8:6-19.

Then, as is notorious, Solomon has a weakness for women: he has 700 wives and 300 concubines, according to 1 Kings 11:3. And the difficulty for our narrator is not so much his sexual appetite as the effect that these women had on him: 'his wives turned his heart to strange gods', we read, and then we are given a description of the ways in which Solomon goes wrong (11:4-13).

The anxiety here is that in some sense the person in the position of leadership stands for the entire nation, so if the king worships gods that are not YHWH, that has an effect on the whole country. This idolatry (for which a regular Old Testament metaphor is that of 'fornication') has the catastrophic effect of sowing the seeds of division in his kingdom. God tells Solomon that it is going to happen (11:13), and then it is foreshadowed in the rebellion of Jeroboam (11:26-36). Significantly, this disaster, which so heavily portends what

---

23. See the terrible stories in 1 Kings 2:12-23, 28-32.

will take place in the future, is the last thing we hear about Solomon, and must constitute the verdict on his leadership. It comes as no surprise when we read the story of Jeroboam's successful rebellion against the inept policies of Solomon's son Rehoboam (12:1-20); that is what happens when those in leadership positions take their eyes off God.

Some questions for reflection
- What are the principal temptations of the people of God with regard to authority?
- Is monarchy a good thing in the people of God?
- In what ways can authority go wrong in the people of God?

CHAPTER SIX

The tension between institution and charism

One thing that has become very evident so far in this book is that the only proper source of authority is God. Yet, at the same time, we need our institutions, and this can lead to a tension between those who claim to have direct experience of God and those who claim that the institution (as it might be the Temple or the priesthood or the monarchy or the Church) carries that experience and is authorised by God. In this chapter I want to explore this tension a little more deeply: the direct knowledge of God and the demands of the institution can be deeply in conflict.

To that end, I offer two examples, taken almost at random from the pages of the Old Testament.

Micaiah ben Imlah (1 Kings 22)

The first is the extraordinary story of Micaiah ben Imlah in 1 Kings 22. It is not often read in church, for obvious reasons, so it may be unfamiliar to some readers. The narrator places this tale in the context of the story of King Ahab and his tensions with Elijah. Ahab came to the throne of Israel, the Northern Kingdom, in about 873 BC, and according to 1 Kings 16:29 reigned for 22 years (though it is hard to be precise about the dates). He was clearly quite a gifted monarch; archaeology reveals that his buildings at Samaria were of a very high standard. He was a serious enough opponent to the Assyrian military expansion to receive a mention in Assyrian chronicles, which tell us that at the battle of Qarqar (853 BC), Ahab had 2000 chariots and 10,000 soldiers.

The biblical author does not concentrate on his talents as a ruler so much as on his behaviour towards God and other people: Ahab is a Bad Thing (16:30-33), partly because he married Jezebel, and in consequence, like Solomon, he drifted in the direction of the worship of other gods, which may well have seemed to him a perfectly sensible political option.[24]

From the outset, therefore, Ahab has a bad press from the Deuteronomic historian, and the tension worsens with the appearance of the mysterious and forbidding figure of Elijah. Elijah appears quite abruptly, fully grown, in the narrative, and threatens Ahab with a drought (17:1) in the name of YHWH God of Israel. Elijah is protected by God, somewhat against the odds (17:3-16), but he survives, with his very direct experience of God. This leads to the famous contest with the prophets of Baal. We must remember as we read that Ahab has built a temple to Baal, and that his wife is significantly the daughter of 'Ethbaal' and is therefore evidently suspected of being on the wrong side. Elijah effortlessly wins the contest and then kills all the prophets of Baal, after which Ahab shows himself a good deal more tractable and does precisely what Elijah tells him (18:41-6).

Mrs Ahab, however (Jezebel, you will recall), is not pleased and threatens to kill Elijah (19:1-3). Elijah seeks refuge in God and is once more rescued by divine intervention (19:3-8). Then he is given enough food to enable him to walk to Horeb, the mountain of God, where he has a very powerful experience of God. This culminates in instructions to become 'involved in politics' by anointing two kings and

---

24. In that culture, if you needed to be allied with particular countries or dynasties, it was very important to worship their deities.

one prophet – his successor Elisha (19:9-18). Elijah disappears for chapters 20 and 22, which is a single narrative and is the story in which we are here interested. The prophet surfaces, however, in chapter 21, in the appalling tale of Naboth's vineyard, in which Jezebel plays such a dominating part as she aims to cheer up her husband by way of perjury and murder when he is distressed at Naboth's refusal to cooperate with his request. So an atmosphere is created in which the prophet's direct experience of God throws down a powerful challenge to the king of Israel; that is the mood in which we arrive at chapter 22.

In this chapter we have a military and political stand-off between Aram (Syria) and the Northern Kingdom of Israel. Ahab is still king in those parts but goes largely unnamed in this chapter. He enters into an alliance with Jehoshaphat, who is now king of the Southern Kingdom of Judah. Israel is more powerful, economically and from the military point of view, and Jehoshaphat needs to make peace with his muscular Northern neighbour. Ahab engages him to join in an expedition against Ramoth-Gilead – a place of some strategic significance on the main road to Damascus – whose ownership was contested between Israel and Syria. Jehoshaphat has no choice but to answer, 'As I am, so are you; as is my people, so is your people; as is my cavalry, so is your cavalry' (22:4), which is diplomatic if not absolutely pellucid. He also adds an exhortation, pious sounding but subversive in intent, that his powerful ally should 'seek today the word of God' (verse 5). Naturally this is an offer not to be refused without grave risk, and so the anonymous king of Israel gathers no less than 400 prophets and puts to them the key question: 'Am I to go up to war against Ramoth-Gilead, or am I not?' (verse 6).

Now these prophets, like too many religious figures down the ages, offer the response that they know the powers-that-be are looking for, and they say, as one voice, 'Go – and YHWH will give it into the hand of the king' (verse 6). Jehoshaphat, however, shows himself to be a man of some courage – or spiritual discernment – and asks for a second opinion: 'Is there no other prophet for YHWH from whom we may enquire?' (verse 7). Then the narrative becomes decidedly interesting, for the king makes a telling response: 'There is still one other man to enquire from YHWH from him; but I hate him, because he does not prophesy good about me but evil: Micaiah ben Imlah' (verse 8). Jehoshaphat makes another diplomatic response: 'Let not the king say so' (verse 8). We already know (as does the anonymous Ahab) how it will turn out, but it is with a certain interest that we hear the king sending an official for Micaiah.

The narrator then depicts quite a dramatic scene (verse 10): 'The King of Israel and Jehoshaphat King of Judah seated each on their throne, clothed in robes at the entrance to the gate of Samaria' (the gate is of course the place where serious business is done in an ancient city), 'and all the prophets were prophesying in their presence'. We are given the impression of a slightly chaotic situation; the reader is presumably meant to imagine the prophets raving and reinforcing their message about going to attack Ramoth-Gilead. Then the narrator draws our attention to one of them, Zedekiah ben Kenaanah, who does some symbolic magic with some iron horns that he has constructed, and roundly declares, 'Thus says YHWH,' (and we know this solemn form of utterance carries a powerful implication that what is predicted will take place) 'with these you shall gore Syria, until you destroy them' (verses 11, 12). All his fellow prophets are giving the same message, which the reader well knows is the message that the king wants to hear. So it will almost certainly be false, and we are invited to reflect on the extent to which the institutional authorities always want God on their side, and put pressure on the charismatic prophets.

Not only that, but the royal official who has been sent to fetch Micaiah tips him the wink to know what is good for him: 'Look out, please: each one of the prophets is prophesying good for the king; let your word be like their word – speak good' (verse 13). Micaiah's response is hardly accommodating: 'As YHWH lives, in accordance with what YHWH says to me, that is what I shall speak.' Once again we feel the tension between the prophet who is in the confidence of God and the official who knows what the king expects. It is therefore something of a shock when we hear Micaiah's first response to the king's request: 'Go up – and you will succeed. The Lord will deliver [Aram] into the hand of the King' (verse 15). There is more to come, however, for, quite unexpectedly, the king refuses to believe him[25] and says, 'How many times am I to put you under oath to tell me only the truth, in the name of the Lord?' (verse 16). Clearly we are meant to understand that the king knows what is going on. Micaiah therefore tells the truth: 'I saw all Israel scattered on the mountains. . .' (verse 17) – a bleak picture that has the ring of authority about it.

The king is not pleased (we do not know whether to be surprised or not), and tells Jehoshaphat, 'Didn't I tell you that that he would not prophesy good of me, but [only] evil?' (verse 18). Micaiah is now in full flow, however, and reveals the vision that he has been granted, of God sending a spirit

---

25. Of course, we cannot hear the tone or see the facial expression with which the prophet makes his utterance, which may have been tongue in cheek.

to Ahab (who is named for the first time in the narrative) to deceive him. The spirit volunteers for the job, and tells God how it is to be done: 'I shall go out and become a lying spirit in the mouth of all his prophets' (verses 19-22).

Naturally the political institution will not readily put up with this unfashionable discourse, and Zedekiah ben Kenaanah slaps Micaiah in the face (verse 24).[26] Ahab orders him to be arrested and put on a starvation diet until the king's return, but Micaiah's only response is, 'If indeed you return in peace, YHWH has not spoken through me' (verse 28). We know what will happen next. And so, indeed, does the king, for he goes into battle in disguise while Jehoshaphat has to wear the full royal uniform. It does not work, though, for Ahab is killed 'and the dogs licked up his blood, and the prostitutes bathed in it, as the word of the Lord which he had spoken' (verse 38).

It is an extraordinary story with many twists and turns, but the underlying message is that God's word has a greater authority than that of any institutional politician, whether a king like Ahab or a prophet like Zedekiah. We are also brought face to face with the temptation to go along with what everyone else is saying. We have reason to be grateful to the editor who decided that this was a tale not to be omitted. There is much to learn here.

Amos and Amaziah (Amos 7:10-17)

The second story that likewise makes this point is the well-known tale of the prophet Amos and his encounter with the priest Amaziah. He is, we must recall, a southerner and therefore a guest in the Northern Kingdom, and he is scarcely

---

26. As a servant of another political authority will do later to Jesus (John 18:22), and yet another to Paul (Acts 23:2).

diplomatic, condemning the prosperity and immorality of Israel. You cannot expect him to get away with this temerity; institutions have a way of getting back at those who attack them. And so it turns out.

The first response on the part of the institution is that Amaziah makes a report to the secular authority – the king; the report, moreover, is false:

> Amos has conspired against you, in the heart of the house of Israel:
> the land cannot bear all his words.
> For this is what Amos has said: 'Jeroboam is going to die by the sword,
> and Israel will certainly be exiled from its soil'.
> *Amos 7:10, 11*

As far as the reader knows, there is not a word of truth in the allegation. The priest, like many in power, is simply looking to sort out an uncomfortable nuisance. In verses 12-13, Amaziah tries to get rid of Amos. His words might literally be translated,

> Run away to the land of Judah, and eat your bread and prophesy there; but at Bethel you are to prophesy no more, for it is the sanctuary of the king and the palace of the kingdom.

In other words, we do not want any of this God-talk here. In response, Amos patiently explains his status: 'I was not a prophet, and I was not a son of a prophet'.[27] Instead, he says, he was a shepherd and tree-dresser, who heard the call of God, 'and the Lord called me from following the flock and the Lord said to me, "Go and prophesy to my people Israel"' (verses 14-15). Then he gives Amaziah the terrible verdict:

---

27. In other words, he does not belong to the prophetic guild.

THE HELPLESSNESS OF GOD

> Now hear YHWH's word: you say, 'You're not to prophesy over Israel', and 'You are not to preach over the House of Isaac'. Therefore thus says the Lord:
> 'Your wife is going to be a prostitute in the city;
> your sons and your daughters shall fall by the sword;
> your land shall be parcelled out by a measuring-line,
> you yourself shall die in an unclean land.
> Israel shall certainly be exiled, not in its own land.'
>
> *Amos 7:16, 17*

This is an appalling thing to hear, and the reader knows that Amaziah has brought it on himself. You mess with the Lord's voice at your own peril. We are all caught within this tension between the institutional and the charismatic, between the call of God and the demands of the institution.

Some questions for reflection
- What does the story of Ahab tell us about leadership in the people of God?
- Are we meant to sympathise with Amaziah or with Amos?
- What can we learn from the tension between prophetic and political authority?

PART TWO

The shape of Jesus' life

Introduction

To sum up where we have been so far: these Old Testament passages about handling authority or leadership roles in the people of God may be seen as the equivalent of the first week of the Ignatian Spiritual Exercises. That is to say they function as stories aimed at encouraging us to face ways in which we and our church operate sinfully when dealing with the exercise of power or authority.

Now we shall continue the process by looking at Jesus' life, through the lens of the second to fourth weeks. The second week takes us from Jesus' birth to his arrival in Jerusalem, and is the moment when we discern whether God is inviting us to make a choice of lifestyle or 'vocation'. The third week has us praying over Jesus' Passion, as a way of confirming whether we really wish to follow him on this way of the cross. The fourth week sees us praying to share Jesus' risen joy, since that is the mood in which we should emerge from retreat and return to our ordinary life.

As we have said, one reason for approaching the material in this way is that our present Bishop of Rome has been formed by this 30-day silent retreat, which he will have made twice in his life as a Jesuit. The suggestion is that his new and fresh way of dealing with the challenges of exercising leadership in the people of God springs from that experience of the Spiritual Exercises, made twice in full and renewed each year in his eight-day annual time with God. It may be of interest to readers to speculate about the difference the Exercises might be said to have made in his spiritual journey. In particular, the shape of the Exercises may serve to model a 'discerning' way of leadership in the Church.

CHAPTER SEVEN

The helplessness of God in the infancy narratives

At the heart of the issue that we are considering – the management of power, or leadership, or authority in the Church (or people of God) – is the nature of the God on whose behalf all such authority is exercised. One of the striking features of the God revealed in the New Testament is, shockingly enough, God's helplessness. This of course has implications for the way leadership is to be exercised among the people of God

St Ignatius picks up something of this in the contemplation that begins the second week proper. You will find this, on the nativity, at Exercises 114,[28] where the retreatant is invited

> to see the persons, i.e. to see Our Lady and Joseph and the servant-girl and the child Jesus, after he has been born, making myself a poor little unworthy little slave, watching them, contemplating them and serving them in their necessities, as though I were present.

You will notice the lack of power implicit in this contemplative role of the 'poor little unworthy little slave',[29] and in this chapter I should like to argue that the lack of power reflects the helplessness that an attentive reader will find in the infancy narratives of both Matthew and Luke.

---

28. It might be useful, though it is not essential, for the reader to have access to the text of the Exercises, for the wider context. You can find an unnumbered and rather ancient translation online at http://www.jesuit.org/jesuits/wp-content/uploads/The-Spiritual-Exercises-.pdf (accessed 30 January 2014). Or a good English edition is *Saint Ignatius Loyola: Personal Writings*, translated with Introductions and Notes by Joseph A. Munitiz and Philip Endean, Penguin Classics, 1996, pp.281-360.
29. Spanish: 'haciéndome yo un pobrecito y esclavito indigno'.

Matthew's infancy narrative

Matthew starts his story in a very unexpected way – with a genealogy. In this prologue he outlines the three stages of Israel's history, from the promise given to Abraham (Matthew 1:2), to the apparent fulfilment of that promise in the brilliant reigns of David and Solomon (1:6) and its denial in the catastrophe of the exile to Babylon, to the climax of the genealogy, which is nothing other than the birth of 'Jesus known as Messiah' (1:16). In other words, in a code that would have been self-evident to his readers or hearers, Matthew is describing the arrival of Jesus as the climax of God's dealing with his people, through all kinds of vicissitudes, including those caused by human infidelity. Matthew even makes the meaning a little clearer by stressing that the three divisions of the genealogy each number 14 (although if you count the third one very carefully you will observe that it only comes to 13!). You can interpret this number in several ways, but clearly Matthew regards it as a very important number and is telling us, in his coded manner, that we are encountering here the perfection of God's dealings.

For our purposes, however, as we look at the question of the exercise of authority or power under God, one important lesson from this genealogy may simply be the daring way in which God puts Godself into our rather uncertain hands. Look, if you like, at all the names in that list of Jesus' ancestors, and where they have a biblical story, chase it up and see what ropey examples of ungodly behaviour quite a lot of them were. Nevertheless, Matthew is quietly telling us, God can work through all that to bring the divine project to its fulfilment.

There is a little more here, too. Somewhat unusually, Matthew mentions four women in this genealogy. They are, in order, Tamar (1:3), Rahab (1:5), Ruth (1:5), and 'Mrs Uriah' (1:6). What is all this about? There are various explanations, but if you read their stories in, respectively, Genesis 38, Joshua 2:1-21, the whole book of Ruth (it is only four charming chapters), and 2 Samuel 11-12, you will see that there are two possible common features to their stories. The first is that their domestic arrangements are all somewhat unusual, and the second is that they may well have been regarded as non-Israelites. Either way, they fit Matthew's purpose of demonstrating that God can write straight with crooked lines – something that we need to remember.

Next we read that 'Mary was found to be pregnant' (1:18). Matthew emphasises that this was before she and Joseph 'came together', which makes it a very shocking discovery, and he delays until the very end of the sentence the information that the child was 'from the Holy Spirit'. So our attention is drawn to Mary and her unenviable situation, which might end in death. However, God is deliberately working through human agency and is therefore helpless to do more than give the occasional nudge to the process.

Not unreasonably, Joseph is determined on a quiet divorce (which is better than insisting on his fiancée being stoned to death), as he is 'reluctant to make an example of her' (verse 19). At this point we recognise that God is in charge, for Matthew introduces the first of five dreams. It is important to be clear, as Matthew tells the story, that any of the dreams might have failed to have the desired effect, for each of them requires human obedience. Once again we see that God's model of leadership or authority is not by way of bullying, but rather by allowing human beings their autonomy; so God is, strictly speaking, quite helpless.

The five dreams, as it turns out, all have their intended effect. The first is an instruction to Joseph (from an angel in a dream – and would *you* have done what Joseph did?) to accept Mary as his wife (1:20-5), and repeats the affirmation that the child is 'from the Holy Spirit'. Instructions are given about the naming of the child, and a Scripture citation is offered (though it is not clear whether this is the evangelist's editorial comment or what the angel says in the dream) which, as it turns out, offers a structure for the entire Gospel (see how 28:20 picks up the idea of 'God with us' from 1:23).

The second dream (2:12) is hardly mentioned at all, but is Matthew's way of getting the Magi off stage and preventing them from giving Herod the information that he requested (2:8), ostensibly so that he might join in worshipping the 'dear little child'. The reader is well aware of what Herod has in mind, and so breathes a sigh of relief when the innocent Magi, who have already shown themselves alert to heavenly revelations, are diverted from going back to Jerusalem. Again, this comes under the category of a divine nudge, but it has the desired effect.

The third dream, which occurs immediately afterwards, contains instructions to Joseph to 'flee to Egypt' (2:13-15). The alert reader knows perfectly well that Egypt is a place *from* which, rather than *to* which, the people of God are supposed to flee, and is correspondingly shocked. For our purposes the point to notice is that, once more, Joseph has a choice. This dream is linked to the previous one that he received by a word that can be translated 'Up you get' (verse 13), which was used in expressing Joseph's obedience to that first dream. Now, however, the situation is urgent, and the mother and the 'dear little child' stand in dire need of protection, 'for Herod is about to seek out the dear little child in order to destroy it' (verse 13). Joseph's obedience is described (using once more the 'getting up' verb) as a kind of reverse of the Exodus: it takes place at night, but we are told that 'he went up to Egypt', which is once again unexpected. This yields the sense of God being in charge, but dependent on human response.

And so to the fourth dream. Once again there is an Exodus, but this time it is headed where it should be, back to the land of Israel (verses 19-21). We may remember as we read it how the previous Exodus depended on the wholehearted response of the people of God, which was not always forthcoming. Once again there is the 'getting up' word, which is repeated when Joseph obeys his instructions, to underline the completeness of his response to God's command. There is also a powerful reminder of the Exodus in the phrase Matthew employs to describe what Joseph has done: 'he entered the land of Israel'.

The final dream is the device by which Joseph is brought into Galilee (verses 22, 23). The evangelist does not make very much of this beyond indicating that it is a way of avoiding Archelaus, son of Herod the Great, who was rather too much of a chip off the old block. Once again for our purposes God is in charge, but absolutely requires human response.

The Magi: an encounter between the powerful and the innocent

Right in the middle of his infancy narrative, Matthew places the story of the Magi, which has so powerfully beguiled the Christian imagination down the centuries (Matthew 2:1-12). I want to argue that it strongly reinforces the sense of the vulnerability of God's project. Matthew manages the narrative with some skill, introducing into the very first line of the story the name of 'Herod the King', which, as Matthew's readers will have known, always means trouble, and then, by way of immediate contrast, the word 'behold', which in Matthew tends to signal that God is active, followed by 'Magi from the East arrived in Jerusalem'.

Now 'Magi' is a term that refers to Persian and Babylonian experts in astrology and oneirology,[30] and in that culture that would not mean that they are quacks, as we might rashly conclude, but experts in what is going on in the world. Certainly in this story they are to be understood as having privileged access to correct conclusions. They are not diplomats, however, and their question, 'Where is the one born King of the Jews?' is not the most tactful one that they could have posed. It is backed up by the statement, 'We saw his star in the East, and have come to worship him', but it could usefully have been thought through a bit more, given that there is a 'King of the Jews' currently reigning, and his name is Herod, and he is somewhat inclined to murder anything that looks as though it might be a threat to his throne.

For our purposes, the interesting fact is that Herod clearly believes their revelation: 'When he heard this, King Herod was disturbed – and all Jerusalem with him', and this starts an important theme of this first Gospel, but he would not have been disturbed had he supposed that these were just charlatans. Indeed he 'gathers together'[31] his religious experts and asks them where the Messiah is to be born. They press the appropriate buttons on their computer and come up with 'Bethlehem', as well as a Scripture quotation to match,

---

30. The interpretation of dreams.
31. The Greek word used for 'gather together' will have reminded Matthew's readers of the word 'synagogue'.

from Micah 5:2. God's project, for those who know a bit about Herod's homicidal paranoia, is at this point quite vulnerable, and that is made very clear in the following sentence: 'Then Herod *secretly* summoned the Magi and found out from them the exact time when the star had appeared.' That word 'secretly' tells it all: he believes that the Messiah has indeed been born, and his intention is to make sure that this 'new kid on the block' does not interfere with his reign.

Herod now appears to be in charge of things and packs the Magi off to Bethlehem, with the sinister injunction, 'Off you go and enquire carefully about the dear little child; and when you find him, let me know, so that I too may come and *worship* him.' The reader knows exactly what Herod has in mind, and 'worship' is not perhaps the best description; so we follow these unsophisticated Magi with some anxiety: are they going to be indiscreet and bring about the premature slaughter of God's Messiah?

We are slightly reassured by what happens next: the star reappears and leads them to where the child is, so God is indeed in control. They 'rejoiced with a very great joy', and that confirms that they are on the right side, as they prove by making their offerings of gold, frankincense and myrrh – luxury gifts fit for a king.[32] It is also possible that the ancient understanding, which is found as early as Irenaeus in the second century – that the three gifts represent Jesus as king, as priest and as destined to die – may also have something in it. They do indeed worship Jesus (verse 11), starting another theme that runs throughout Matthew's Gospel.

---

32. The fact that they brought three gifts is why it is traditionally thought there were just three Magi – but in fact Matthew does not tell us the size of the expedition, which could have been anything from two upwards; the upper limit would be a party that might have been regarded as a hostile invasion.

Meanwhile, the reader is still worrying about what is going to happen when they go back to Jerusalem: are they going to tell Herod precisely where to find the one born as Messiah? But, once again, God gives the situation a nudge, and (as we have seen) the Magi are sent home by another route. So we breathe again, although we are not surprised to read in chapter 2:16-18 that Herod then murdered 'all the children that were in Bethlehem and the surrounding area, of two years old and under'. However (as Paul remarked in another context: see 1 Corinthians 1:25), the helplessness of God triumphs over human aggression, and the child lives to see Egypt and eventually, as the reader is sadly aware, the cross in Jerusalem. The Magi, and not Herod, are on the right side.

Luke's infancy narrative

It seems good to start this section by drawing attention to a characteristic tactic of Luke – what we may like to call his 'three-card trick'. If we leave out of account his introduction to the Gospel (Luke 1:1-4), we see that each of his first three chapters begins with a sentence where Luke allows us to look at the powerful, only to make us realise that they are not, after all, the most important in his scheme of things. In the first place, at 1:5, like Matthew, he uses the phrase 'in the days of Herod the King' before letting us see that, after all, it is not that consummate politician and friend of Rome in whom Luke is interested, but two very ordinary members of priestly families, whose unimportance is underlined by the fact that they are childless (1:5-7) – namely Zachariah and his wife Elizabeth. Nevertheless, it is those unimportant and helpless ones who are to carry on God's vulnerable project, and it is to Zachariah that the angel Gabriel makes his appearance 'on the right hand side of the altar of incense' (verse 11).

Secondly, at the beginning of chapter 2, Luke deliberately imitates the style of an ancient historian, once again with the apparent intention of making us look at the powerful:

> It happened in those days that a decree went out from Caesar Augustus that the entire inhabited world should be registered. This registration was the first that took place when Quirinius was the Procurator of Syria.

Then we hear the effect of this bureaucratic decision, made by those in power far away in Rome, on all the ordinary people: 'And they all started to journey to get registered, each one in their own city' (verse 3). The point to notice here is that word that I have translated as 'journey'. It is a favourite word of Luke,[33] and although the sentence describes the awfulness inflicted by central authority on ordinary people,[34] that word 'journey' is Luke's way of expressing that the whole of Luke–Acts (for we have to think of it as a single story in two volumes) is a 'journey'. It is a one which encounters many obstacles, but in the end it reaches its destination[35] because it is a journey that is driven by the Spirit. At this early stage of the story the reader is not yet wised up to this, but it becomes clear in verse 4 that the people who interest Luke are not the Emperor of Rome, nor his local representative, but Joseph and Mary, whom we have already met in the first chapter of the Gospel. Mary is introduced here as Joseph's fiancée, with the shocking intelligence that she is pregnant. Not only therefore are they at the mercy of faraway potentates; not only is Mary in a

---
33. From the Greek *poreuomai*.
34. Consider, if you like, the queues for immigration at Heathrow on many days of the week.
35. Rome – that is to say, the entire world.

delicate condition as she makes this involuntary journey; worse than either of these is the fact that she is pregnant when she should not be.

Thirdly, and this is the most extreme example, consider the beginning of chapter 3. Once again, Luke takes up the pen of a professional historian, and even gives a date (the only one in the entire New Testament) as he writes, impressively:

> In the fifteenth year of the imperium of Tiberius Caesar, when Pontius Pilatus was procurator of Judea, and Herod was tetrarch of Galilee, and his brother Philip was tetrarch of the region of Ituraea and Trachonitis, and Lysanias was tetrarch of Abilene, in the high-priesthood of Annas and Caiaphas . . .

Then, just as we are reflecting, not only on how these are the most important persons in the world as the focus of Luke's sentence narrows from Rome to Palestine, but also on what an unpleasant shower they are and how little you would like to meet them on a dark night, Luke reveals the one in whom he is really interested, as he concludes, sharpening his focus, 'the word of God came to [none of these unsavoury personages but to] John, the son of Zechariah – in the desert!'

This three-card trick is Luke's rather subtle way of indicating who the people are who really matter in God's project, and, oddly enough, they are not the Roman emperor, nor his local representatives, nor any of the people who appear to hold the power, but the weird son of a Temple priest, living where human beings do not live, in the desert. It is a very odd tale, and one that we should bear in mind as we read the rest of this Gospel.

For the moment it will be enough to see the vulnerability of God's project as we read through the remainder of the two opening chapters. Many readers are struck by the artistic way in which Luke implicitly asserts the total unimportance of Mary (1:26, 27). The evangelist links her into the previous episode by using the phrase 'in the sixth month' (which will be explained in verse 56 – 'about three months'), and then goes on to say who she is, in a way that puts her right at the end as Luke sharpens his focus. He begins with the word 'was sent', which his readers will have easily translated as 'God sent', and then we find out who is given this mission: 'the angel Gabriel'. Then the destination of the mission is revealed, in rather general terms: 'a city of the Galilee'. Next we are given its rather obscure name 'whose name is Nazareth'. The obscurity is hinted at in the jeering of Nathanael in John 1:46, and by the fact that the city is never mentioned in the entire Old Testament. After this we are given the status of the person to whom Gabriel is sent: 'a virgin' – in other words, a thoroughly insignificant person, not yet a wife or a mother so that she can be given status. She is, however, 'engaged' (verse 27), and we are told her fiancé's name: 'a man whose name is Joseph, of the house of David'. Only then, and right at the very end of the sentence, does Luke reveal her name: 'and the name of the virgin was Miriam'. And yet the length of the narrative given to the encounter between this insignificant virgin and the angel Gabriel sent from God actually tells us that this meeting is absolutely at the heart of what the evangelist is doing.

This unimportant girl is going to bring forth a child who is at the heart of the story; indeed, he is the subject of the Gospel:

> This one is going to be big;
> and the Lord God is going to give him the throne of David his ancestor,

and he is to be Emperor over the House of Jacob forever;
and of his Empire there shall be no end.
Luke 1:32, 33

It is with some anxiety, therefore, that we wait for Mary's response, and we must take that seriously as we ponder the helplessness of God, who cannot force her into accepting his project. It follows that we hear her answer with relief (verse 38): 'Look – the Lord's slave-girl', and the use of that last word is a healthy reminder of how we are supposed to operate within the people of God.

The next episode is the encounter of two spirited women – Mary and Elizabeth (verses 43, 44). We do not need to be told that this is a very odd fact, in a society where women were deemed to be at the bottom of the pile, but it is clear that we are intended to applaud Mary who made this long journey, apparently on her own, and Elizabeth who accepted her. We also notice that Elizabeth, 'filled with the Spirit' (verses 41), successfully identified Jesus, with the remarkable proclamation, 'Where does this come from to me that the mother of my Lord should come to me?' (verse 43); so we should applaud her too. And it is worth pointing out that 'the Lord' up to this point in Luke's Gospel has referred unambiguously to God (see 1:6, 9, 11, 15, 16, 17, 25, 32, 38; and compare also 45, 46, 58, 66, 68, 76). So it is a very grand claim that Elizabeth is making here – one that is right at the heart of God's project.

Under these circumstances – of God's helplessness and the lack of power on the part of those who are invited (and willing) to help in the project – we should not be surprised by the song of Mary's subversive joy that follows this episode (1:46-55). It begins, 'My soul makes the Lord great', which is of course no more than it should be, but we should look closely at some of the ideas that it plays with. God is praised because:

- He has looked on the humiliation of his *slave-girl* (verse 48). (This is the second time we have met this word in the Lucan narrative.)
- He has scattered those who are arrogant in the intellects of their hearts (verse 51).
- He has pulled down rulers from their positions of authority, and has lifted up the humble (verse 52).
- He has filled the starving with good things – but the affluent he has sent away hungry (verse 53).

It is said that this song has been banned in various totalitarian states because it is too upsetting for the status quo.

It is of a piece with this that we now return to a very high-spirited woman who is not prepared to be battered down by her male relatives. We have already seen Elizabeth correctly identifying Mary's offspring (1:43); now she overrules those who (taking advantage of Zachariah's current inability to speak) want to name her child after its father. Elizabeth, his mother, roundly objects: 'No – he is going to be called John' (verses 59-64 – and we may reflect that this is appropriate enough, given that the name means 'God has acted graciously'). Her adversaries make the tribal point that 'no one in your family is called that'. They bring Zachariah into the question and (perhaps pardonably forgetting that he is dumb, not deaf) 'they signalled to him, what did he want the child to be called?' Zachariah equips himself with an iPad or some such thing and makes it clear that 'John is his name'. As well they might be, 'they were all astonished'. Again we marvel at the small ways in which God's project is advanced, despite the strength of opposition to it.

THE HELPLESSNESS OF GOD

We have already (when considering 3:1, 2) mentioned the comparative unimportance of the child who is given this name of John, but he is found in the desert, not where (we naively assume) the action is. Now Luke deposits him there, and we are aware that, beneath the surface of the text, God is in charge: 'the little child grew, and grew strong in the Spirit. And he was in the desert, until the days of his manifestation before Israel' (1:80).

From there, Luke moves us, by way of the decree from Caesar Augustus to which we have already referred (2:1-5), and the command of the powerful has a remarkable effect on God's project. Look now at the manner in which Luke describes what happens next – the helplessness of the birth of the infant that is God's final throw of the dice:

> It happened when they were there [in Bethlehem] the days were fulfilled for her to give birth. And she brought forth her son, the first-born, and she wrapped him up in swaddling-cloths, and laid him down in a dog-bowl – because there was no room for them in the lodging.
>
> *Luke 2:6, 7*

There are three words in this account to which we should pay attention. The first is 'fulfilled'. The clear implication is that God is in charge, even in these unlikely circumstances. The second is the word 'dog-bowl', which is perhaps just a little tendentious as a translation. The word really means a 'feeding-trough' – a place where animals browse – to which tradition has given the Norman French word 'manger', but that has become too familiar and insufficiently shocking. The third is 'the lodging', from which Joseph and Mary and their offspring are excluded. That is likewise rather shocking: ancient Near Eastern culture is instinctively open to guests, especially when there is the danger of an imminent birth. Furthermore, the word I have translated as 'lodging' is a very general term – one that can mean, for example, a place where camels are untied, but also an inn.

So this new child, of which we have heard so much in chapter 1, and which is God's project ('Emperor over the House of Jacob forever'), is now found in the helplessness of new birth and lying in a feeding-trough (or dog-bowl), and excluded from even the most basic hospitality. We shiver at the discomfort and the implicit menace to what God is attempting. Not only that, but with the next episode, 'there goes the neighbourhood', as they say. For in 2:8-20 we meet the divinely appointed witnesses to the birth of the one who has been described to us as 'Saviour' (borrowing for the purpose a title that Caesar Augustus had made his own). They are 'shepherds', and we must not think here of pastoral idylls or rural tranquillity. These people, to whom the 'angel of the Lord' appears (and that is how we know that they are divinely appointed witnesses), are not at all respectable; they are so beyond the pale that they are working at night. The nearest equivalent might be American cowboys, readier to shoot than to answer questions.

Nevertheless, it is to these unlikely people that 'the angel of the Lord' appears and whom 'the glory of the Lord shone around' (2:9), and they show that (surprisingly, given their social level) 'they feared a great fear', which is a clear sign that they are open to what God is about. Then, like a host of Old Testament witnesses, they are told, in good biblical language,

> Do not be afraid: look!
> I am gospelling you a great joy which is for all the people;
> because a child has been born for you today,
> who is Christ the Lord,
> in the city of David.
>
> *Luke 2:10, 11*

This is a thoroughly unpromising beginning for God's project, but somehow the reader just knows that all will be well, even if there will be some rough passages on the way. One word to notice here is the word 'today'. It is a word of which Luke makes impressive use, and its function is to underline the unexpectedness of God's action. It appears ten times in the Gospel of Luke; we shall not cite them all here, but the reader may be interested in the following instances:

- In 4:21 it is one of the words in Jesus' commendably brief sermon in Nazareth: '*Today*, these things are fulfilled in your hearing', where it refers to the unexpected fulfilment of Isaiah 61:1, 2 in Jesus' mission.
- In 5:26 it is the verdict of the people on Jesus' implicit claim to be able to forgive sins when the crippled man is let down through the roof: 'We have seen remarkable things *today*', they exclaim, vindicating God's project.
- The word is used twice in the Zacchaeus story (19:5, 9), where it is a sign that God's 'salvation', which has already been mentioned (1:69, 71, 77) as that which God is bringing in the person of Jesus, has come to a thoroughly unexpected person – certainly one who is no better than those shepherds back in chapter 1. There are two uses of 'today' in this episode – first when Jesus announces quite unexpectedly that '*today* I must stay in your house' (and we should remember that Luke is a Gospel in which hospitality has a very high value), and '*today* salvation has come to this house'.
- The final use of the word is perhaps the most unexpected of all, for it is addressed to a criminal on the cross who has improbably addressed the dying Jesus as 'Emperor': 'Jesus – remember me when you come into your Empire', he

says, and is given the astonishing response: 'Amen I'm telling you: *today* you're going to be with me in Paradise' (23:42, 43).

The freshness of Luke's Gospel comes from the sheer unexpectedness of the project of God that it recounts, and the evangelist's use of the innocent-looking little word 'today' is an apt vehicle for it.

The next episode (2:22-38) confirms this impression. It is the story of Jesus' presentation in the Temple, with the offering that is prescribed for the poor rather than the well-to-do ('a pair of turtle-doves or two young doves' – see Leviticus 12:8), which is rather odd for the parents of the future emperor. Not only that, but once again those who are chosen as witnesses to the 'Christ of the Lord' are not the important people. Instead we meet two humble characters who have stepped straight out of the pages of the Old Testament. The first of these is Symeon, 'just and pious and waiting for the comfort of Israel' who, like Mary earlier, describes himself as a 'slave' (verse 29), and attests that this unpromising and far from wealthy infant is indeed God's 'saving thing' (verse 30). There is no doubt at all that this elderly religious person has correctly identified what is going on: 'Look! This one is placed for the fall and rising of many in Israel, and a sign that is being contradicted'. Then he adds, this time directly to Mary, 'and as for you yourself, a sword is going to pierce your heart' (verses 34, 35). So we reflect, sad but not altogether surprised, that this Messiah is bringing contradiction and pain; but he is nevertheless God's Messiah (verses 26, 28, 30-2).

Then we meet the second witness, namely Hannah, apparently equally elderly and religious, who adds her contribution: 'she praised God and started speaking about him [that is, presumably, either God or Jesus] to all those who were waiting for the redemption of Jerusalem' (verse 38).

These two witnesses might seem unimportant when set against the Caesars, Augustus and Tiberius; but they have it right, and they know what God's project is about. God is in charge, we dimly grasp, but not with the massed bands of the big battalions. Luke underlines this important lesson in the next episode, after the presentation of Jesus in the Temple:

> And when they had perfected everything according to the Law of the Lord, they returned to the Galilee, to their city of Nazareth. And the child grew and became strong, filled with wisdom – and God's grace was on him.
>
> *Luke 2:39, 40*

We have established that this child is indeed God's Messiah, the Emperor, God's salvation, God's project; but he remains only a child, and like all children, he has to grow slowly. God is in no hurry. The text starts by reminding us that Joseph and Mary have done what they are supposed to do. Then they return to Galilee, which few of Luke's readers will ever have heard of, to Nazareth, which no one has ever heard of. And why? For the child to grow! God is biding his time. All is well, nevertheless, because as with his mother (1:28), 'God's grace was upon him'. This is God's project, even if it is on the slow burner.

There is a brief moment of anxiety when the boy asserts himself (verses 41-52) and resembles, as I once heard a preacher say, 'every adolescent you ever knew: lippy, self-absorbed and antagonistic to his parents'. That may not be quite what Luke is saying, but it is a striking story, this of Jesus staying in Jerusalem for three days after the celebration of the Passover and interrogating 'the teachers'. This evokes some tension with his parents, as his mother reproaches him for the agony that 'your father and I have endured'. He in turn reproaches her: 'So why were you looking for me? Didn't you realise . . . ?' And this fact, so clear to him but obscure to Mary and Joseph, is that 'it was inevitable that I should be on my Father's affairs'. This remark asserts the absolute priority of what we are calling 'God's project', and at the same time, perhaps rather painfully, it redefines Jesus' family so that it is not Joseph but God who is to be called his 'Father'.

We may feel at this point that the project has a somewhat uncertain future, so it is with some relief that we notice the next move in the dance: 'he went down with them and came to Nazareth, and was subordinated to them'; so he had found his place in the family structure. He was 12 (verse 42), Luke thinks, when this took place, and he was about 30 when he finally started on his mission (3:23); once again, therefore, we see that God is in no hurry to develop the project.

This lack of hurry appears also in two other texts in this Lucan infancy narrative. On the face of it, they are about what Mary does, but I think that they are also signals to the reader as to what we are to do with the events that occur in these infancy narratives. They read as follows:

- And Mary was keeping these events to herself, pondering them in her heart (2:19)
- And his mother was keeping all these events in her heart (2:51)

There is much to ponder here, not least the nature of God's project.

Some questions for reflection
- Do you see signs of the 'helplessness of God' in the infancy narratives of Matthew and Luke?
- Are there any hints here of how leadership should be exercised in the people of God?
- Why do you think Matthew and Luke opted to start their Gospels with an 'infancy narrative'?

CHAPTER EIGHT

'Authority' in Jesus' ministry

In the second week of the Spiritual Exercises of St Ignatius, the retreatant is invited to follow the life and ministry of Jesus, starting with his birth. We have looked at the two Gospel narratives of his birth in chapter 7. The second week now continues as we follow the events of Jesus' life all the way through to the eve of Palm Sunday.

In this chapter I should like to look at the way in which Jesus exercises authority, and to find there the model which we have been calling in this book the 'helplessness of God'. There is not space here to examine every Gospel narrative. Instead I propose to take two of the evangelists and explore, in Mark's case, the idea of authority that is so important in his Gospel, and, in the case of Matthew, what the Sermon on the Mount can tell us about God's project. What I am arguing in this chapter is the general thesis that the source of Jesus' power, and therefore of that of his disciples, is in the helplessness of God; it is therefore utterly subversive of all human power, and requires us to embrace weakness.

Mark's Gospel and authority

The fundamental perception of the second evangelist is that Jesus has authority that is given to him by God, and, because of God's helplessness, it ends in Jesus' death. There are two closely related words that Mark uses for this idea. The first is a verb (*exesti*), which means 'it is permitted'; and the second is a noun (*exousia*) derived from that verb, which is best translated as 'authority'. I shall take these two words in the order in which they appear in the Gospel.

The first occurrence is at 1:22, where we find Jesus in the synagogue at Capernaum on the Sabbath. Mark allows us to overhear the comments of an undefined 'they', who 'were thunderstruck at his teaching; for he was teaching them as one who has authority, and not like the scribes'. A wedge is obviously being driven here between Jesus and the scribes, though it does not precisely say how Jesus' teaching might differ from that of the religious experts. It is probably important to point out that the 'scribes' would be those who had the (in that world) rare gift of being able not only to make intelligible marks on papyrus but also to read such marks, and therefore they were able to determine what the Law actually says and what it might be thought to mean. This kind of teaching is a precious gift, but for Mark, Jesus' teaching is different, and implicitly superior. If you were to press Mark to indicate the source of Jesus' authority, he would undoubtedly respond that it was from God.

The second use of the word opens up a new dimension. In 1:26, Jesus has effortlessly commanded an unclean spirit that has (correctly) identified him as 'the Holy One of God' to 'Shut up and come out of him'. With a final convulsion, and a loud shout, it does so. Mark records the effect on Jesus' audience; they are not precisely identified, but we are presumably to think of them as those in the synagogue (1:27):

> They were, every one of them, astonished with the result that they argued among themselves, saying, 'What's this? A new teaching, done with authority! He even gives orders to unclean spirits, and they obey him!'

Once again, the authority is clearly of God, and we are invited to rejoice in the victory.

Not much sign here, you may argue, of the 'helplessness of God'. But wait: there is more to come. In the next episode where we meet the word (2:1-12), there is a potentially lethal accusation which is going to surface later in Jesus' life. As always in the first half of Mark's Gospel, there are wall-to-wall crowds as Jesus 'speaks the message to them', so some people who were 'bringing a paralytic to him, carried by four', are forced to attempt the unorthodox solution of 'unroofing the roof where he was' (2:3, 4). Jesus' response is as authoritative as ever, but slightly unexpected: 'Child – your sins are forgiven'. At this point we discover that there are scribes among those present, and Mark does not allow us to dwell on the unlikeliness of that, as we overhear them muttering to themselves:

Why does this one talk like this? He is blaspheming!
Who can forgive sins, except one, namely God?
Mark 2:7

They are asking a good question, as is often the case with Jesus' enemies.

There are three points to notice here. First there is the accusation of blasphemy (verse 7), which will be repeated by the High Priest in Jesus' trial at 14:64, where such an accusation would be sufficient to obtain a capital verdict. Already, therefore, this reeks of a threat to Jesus' life. The second thing to notice is the word 'can': here (and we shall see this elsewhere) it is a question about authority. Thirdly, the phrase 'except one, namely God' reappears, but on Jesus' lips, at 10:18 where it refers to the question that has been put to Jesus by the rich person (the 'bumptious pietist') who wants to know how to 'inherit eternal life'. The sympathetic reader will read all three of these passages as indicating that, for Mark, Jesus is invested with precisely the authority that God possesses. And it is significant that this authority will lead to his death. The episode ends with a dramatic display of Jesus' authority, and a use of the word (in case we had missed the point of the story):

> Jesus immediately knew in his spirit that they were arguing like this in their hearts, and says to them: 'Why are you making these arguments in your hearts? Which is easier: to say to the paralytic, 'Your sins are forgiven' or to say, 'Up you get and take up your stretcher, and walk?' But, in order that you may know that the Son of Man has *authority* to forgive sins on earth (he says to the paralytic), I am telling you: up you get, take up your stretcher, and go to your house'. And he got up and immediately took up his stretcher and went out before all of them, so that they were all amazed and praised God . . .
>
> *Mark 2:8-12*

That result – not only the healing, but more importantly the resultant praise to God – is clearly seen by Mark as vindicating Jesus' authority to forgive sins. We do not need, however, to be told that this authority is not going to win Jesus any friends.

This becomes even clearer the next time the verb 'it is permitted' is used (2:26). It is on the lips of Pharisees. By now we expect trouble when they appear, for we met them earlier in the chapter in the form of 'the scribes of the Pharisees' (2:16) who objected to Jesus' dreadful dinner companions. Following this there is a complaint, possibly from the Pharisees or from John's disciples, about Jesus' disciples not fasting (2:18). In response, Jesus twice uses the word 'can', clearly referring to what is acceptable behaviour (2:19).

So there is a menacing sense of tension when the disciples are dim-witted enough to pluck ears of corn on the Sabbath, and the Pharisees challenge him directly: 'Look! They're doing what is not permitted *(exesti)* on the Sabbath'. Jesus, never at a loss, and always ready for an original piece of scriptural exegesis, flings the charge back at them and quotes an Old Testament instance when the law was broken (verses 25, 26). Then he concludes with a devastating remark, which will not commend his authority to his opponents: 'the Son of Man is Lord even of the Sabbath'. Here we are very near indeed to the source of Jesus' authority for Mark, and the implicit claim makes his death almost inevitable. Mark is accustoming us to the 'helplessness of God'.

This becomes clear on the next occasion when this verb is used (Mark 3:1-6). Jesus is once more in the synagogue and is presented with a 'person with a withered hand'. Not only that, however, but we learn that 'they were watching him, to see if on the Sabbath he would heal him – so that they could make an accusation against him'. So the situation is fraught and loaded, and there is an implicit question about what is permitted *(exesti)* on the Sabbath. As usual, Jesus attacks the question head on, with no diplomatic nicety. He does it in two stages. First, he orders the man to 'Rise up[36] into the middle.' Then, with our attention on the unfortunate person, he clarifies the agenda: 'Is it permitted *(exesti)* on the Sabbath to do good or to do evil? To save a life or to kill?' It is, that is to say, a question about authority, and he answers that question first: 'and looking round at them with anger, grieving at the hardness of their hearts'. Then he goes on to answer the original question – 'can Jesus heal this man's condition?' – without any effort at all; he just commands the man, 'Stretch out your hand', which he does 'and his hand was restored'. It is as simple as that.

---

36. Here, significantly, he is using Mark's resurrection word.

THE HELPLESSNESS OF GOD

Mark has offered us a very dramatic account of Jesus' ability to heal, and of his authority to do so on the Sabbath. We have to be reminded, however, of the helplessness of God's project, and that is the all-important lesson of the final sentence of the story (verse 6): 'The Pharisees went out immediately and with the Herodians made a decree against him, how they might destroy him.' The Pharisees are odd bedfellows with the Herodians: they stood for independent nationalism while the Herodians presumably represented those who opted for accommodation with Rome. The two of them will come together again at 12:13, when they ask the potentially lethal question about whether or not to pay tax to Caesar. Once again, it seems inevitable that God's project will end in death.

The next use of the word 'authority' (*exousia*) is at 3:14, 15, where the Twelve are appointed, and we learn that they have three functions: 'to be with him; for him to send them to preach; and to have *authority* to expel demons'. So they are to enter into complete solidarity with Jesus' project (and at 6:7 we learn that they are given this same *exousia* as they go out to preach), which means, presumably, that they can be expected to share in its helplessness and vulnerability and might therefore be expected to die like Jesus.

However, as is well known, the disciples do not always get it right in Mark's Gospel. Our next episode is a particular instance of their getting it wrong. Strictly speaking, the narrative (10:35-45) does not mention *exousia* or *exesti*, but the idea is lurking below the surface of the text. The story is that the sons of Zebedee make a bid for power, asking Jesus for a blank cheque,[37] which they express in terms of 'sitting, one on your right and one on your left, in your glory'. Clearly

---

37. Verse 35 – 'we want you to do for us whatever we ask you'.

this request takes no account of what we are calling the 'helplessness of God', as Jesus gently explains ('You do not know what you are asking'). Jesus then rephrases their request in terms of 'cup' and 'baptism', introducing them with the word 'to be able' ('Are you able to drink . . .?'), which we saw previously on the lips of the scribes accusing Jesus of blasphemy with regard to forgiving sins (2:7). The two brothers are ready to accept any condition and fail to realise that the 'cup' and 'baptism' end in death, as they babble, 'We can,' in answer to Jesus' question. At that point Jesus indicates that it is not his job to assort those who sit on his right and on his left.[38]

There is a more important point here, that secular authority operates (as has been too often the case in the Christian churches) in terms of 'lording it over' and 'exercising authority over'. Those ideas have nothing to do with God's project. Instead, Jesus redefines the task of collaboration in God's project in terms of 'service' (verse 43) and 'slavery' (verse 44), and ends with a saying that has resounded down the centuries, although, sadly, without always being heard by Christians who exercise authority: 'For the Son of Man did not come to be served, but to serve – and to give his life as a ransom for many' (verse 45). That is what is meant by the helplessness of God.

In Mark 11:27-33 the question of authority surfaces as potentially lethal. It is the response of the religious establishment to Jesus' shocking behaviour of expelling the stallholders in the Temple and turning over the tables (11:15-17). Their reaction, once more, is that 'they started to look for ways of destroying him' (verse 18).

---

38. And the reader will discover at 15:27 that the people who will eventually be put there are a couple of thieves!

From here on the tension rises: in verses 20-21 we discover that the cursed fig tree – surely a symbol of the corrupt establishment – has obediently withered. Next the establishment confronts him with the question about *exousia*: 'By what authority do you do these things?' Jesus responds with something of a trap about the authority of John the Baptist, which silences them, but it does not bring their homicidal plotting to an end, as Jesus answers in response to their refusal to answer his question, 'Neither am I telling you by what *exousia* I am doing these things.' This leads straight into the parable of the vineyard and the tenants (12:1-12), which clearly has to do with the helplessness of God in the face of human reaction, for it represents the owner of the vineyard as eventually losing not just his servants but also his son to the uncooperative tenants. Then (verses 13-27) comes the 'lethal question', already referred to, about paying taxes to Caesar, and an equally complex legal problem about marriage and the afterlife. The atmosphere becomes more and more sinister until it is evident that death is the only way out. The prediction of the destruction of the Temple (chapter 13) only increases the bleakness of the mood.

Finally, ecclesial authority is vindicated, but only in the context of death and failure (16:5-8). The 'young man' who greets the women inside the tomb instructs them to 'go and tell his disciples – and Peter – that 'he is going before you into the Galilee, and you will see him there'. This is neatly done: the disciples were last seen disappearing in a panic, and Peter is mentioned because, as Jesus previously predicted, he denied ever having heard of his Lord. But the reader knows that they are going to form the basis of the Jesus movement; cowards though they undoubtedly are, God is prepared to entrust the project to them. And, in case we have forgotten the helplessness of God, Mark concludes his Gospel with an account of the women's response to their commission: 'They went out and fled from the tomb, for fear and astonishment had seized them. And they said nothing to nobody – for they were afraid'. There is no room here for power plays in the life of the Church.

Matthew's greatest composition: chapters 5–7

The other example of Jesus' exercise of authority that we shall look at (as a model for the way leadership should be exercised in the Jesus movement) is the Sermon on the Mount. Those who have ever attempted to work out its structure will know how difficult it is to grasp. From the electrifying beginning – those remarkable beatitudes (5:1-12: 'Congratulations to the poor in spirit . . .') – to the puzzling ending, and two parables about how to build a house (7:24-7), it is hard to pin down. Underlying the difficulty is the uncertainty that the reader feels about whether the Sermon is addressed to the disciples only (5:1, 2) or to the crowds (as seems to be implied at 7:28). The teaching is very demanding, but the reader will not be surprised to learn that I should like to suggest that this best of all of Matthew's compositions gains much of its power from what we have been calling the 'helplessness of God'.

The best place to start might be the very awkward middle of this remarkable piece of writing. At verses 1-18 of chapter 6 the reader detects a pattern, where the evangelist talks about the three great pillars of Jewish religious practice: almsgiving (6:1-4), prayer (6:5-14) and fasting (6:16-18). He evidently thoroughly approves of them, but warns his hearers to do them not for show, 'like the actors/hypocrites', so as to be glorified by human beings (2, 5, 16), but 'in secret' (4, 6, 18), where 'your heavenly Father will pay you back'.

At this point we may be asking, if we have forgotten about the helplessness of God, 'In that case, what's the point of it all?' However, we notice that the apparently tidy pattern is broken up by the middle section, on prayer, where Matthew inserts rather violently the prayer that we call the 'Lord's Prayer' (and Matthew's version is the one that most of us know). You may already have noticed that the number of verses assigned to this middle section on prayer is far in excess of what is given to the other two. What you may not have observed is that this section, including the 'Our Father', comes right at the centre of these three chapters, and I want to suggest to you that it is this profound message of the Fatherhood of God that offers a structure for the Sermon. All the teaching it contains comes back to the fact that God is a loving (if helpless) parent, and therefore the recipients of the sermon, whether crowds or disciples, have nothing to fear.

Now let us look at the sermon as a whole. We start with the unforgettable beginning (5:1-11), and I want to suggest that it is only if God is really 'Father' that we can make sense of these unlikely 'congratulations'. Only under those circumstances is it possible for Jesus to offer credibly his felicitations to those improbable categories – of 'poor in spirit', 'those who mourn', 'the meek', 'those who hunger and thirst for justice', 'the merciful',[39] 'the pure in heart', 'the peacemakers', and 'those persecuted for the sake of righteousness'. Only if it is true – which is what Jesus detects in his own experience, that the maker of the universe can properly be understood as a loving parent – can we make

---

39. Those, that is to say, who behave after the manner commended by the great Matthean parable of the absurdly generous king in Matthew 18:21-35.

sense of congratulations offered to this unlikely list of no-hopers. Likewise, only if it is true is it possible for Jesus' disciples to perform their function of 'salt of the earth' and 'light of the world' (5:13-16).

The next part of the Sermon is what scholars call the 'great antitheses' – six sayings of the form, 'You have heard it said ... but I say to you ...' In each case, Jesus implicitly affirms his authority over God's Law, not by decrying that Law but by drawing out its exigencies, and especially the inner discipline that it requires.

Now it is true that the text does not precisely say that this is because of the fatherhood of God; all we can say is that the use of the divine passive – 'it was said' – clearly implies that it is God's word, and that Jesus is entitled to expound the meaning of it. There is more to it than that, for in the last of the six antitheses, quite suddenly (5:45), we find the first in a sudden concentration of uses of the phrase 'your Father, the one in the heavens'. This opens up the theme of God as Father; the hearers are told to be 'perfect, like your Father, the heavenly one, is perfect' (5:48); then, when he starts on the three staples of Jewish piety that we referred to above (almsgiving, prayer and fasting), the references to the Father come thick and fast:

- 6:1 your *plural* Father, the one in heaven
- 6:4 your *singular* Father, who sees in secret
- 6:6 your *singular* Father, who is in secret
- 6:8 your *plural* Father knows what you need
- 6:9: the prayer to our *plural* Father (which is, as we have said, at the very centre of the Sermon on the Mount)
- 6:14 your *plural* Father, the heavenly one
- 6:15 your *plural* Father will forgive
- 6:18 your *singular* Father x 2

- 6:26 your *plural* heavenly Father (feeds the birds of the heaven)
- 6:32 your *plural* Father, the heavenly one (knows your needs)
- 7:11 your *plural* Father in Heaven (will give good gifts)
- 7:21 the will of *my* Father (rather than 'Lord, Lord')

Normally the 'your' here is plural, but in 6:4, 6 and 18 it is singular because in each case it refers to the private, explicitly not public, interaction between the individual and God. In all the other cases there is an implicit assertion that the fatherhood of God means, first, that disciples are all brothers and sisters; and, second, that they have nothing to worry about.

This concentration of references to the Father right in the centre of the Sermon on the Mount has an effect on the reader, so that what looks like a somewhat unstructured set of teachings finds its mooring in the paternal benevolence of God. This means that Jesus' disciples do not have to build up treasure on earth (6:19-21), they can afford to allow God's light into themselves (6:22, 23), can serve the God who is Father rather than the pseudo-god that is Mammon (6:24), have nothing to worry about (6:25-34), and have no call to judge the children of the Father (7:1-6). They can be sure that the Father pays attention to their prayers (7:7-12), that the narrow gate is the one to take (7:13, 14), that fake-prophets do not bring forth the good fruit that one can expect of children of the Father (7:15-20) and, finally, that the only thing that matters is 'doing the will of my Father in heaven' (7:21-3). This is then robustly backed up by the two parables mentioned earlier, about building, respectively, on rock and on sand. Under the circumstances, these must surely refer to the parenthood of God that structures the entire Sermon.

How does that fit with the 'helplessness of God'? It is not explicitly mentioned, I have to admit, but the Sermon on the Mount offers its hearer or reader a choice. We can refuse to respond to the high standards that God offers us, and if we refuse, then there is nothing that God can do beyond the occasional gentle nudge. Or we can accept them, and God can only watch and wait to see what we shall do. That is helplessness of a remarkable sort.

What has this chapter revealed to us? Firstly that Jesus is subversive of power and shows up our temptations to dominate and manipulate. By contrast, he teaches us that the only thing that matters is attention to the Father, not seeking to dominate. This is the context in which the 'choice' or 'election' or 'decision' is made in the second week of the Spiritual Exercises. It builds on the experience of the first week, during the course of which the retreatant has learned the importance of keeping an eye open for unworthy motivation, which is always lurking as a possibility in the background. We are invited to embrace the helplessness of God.

Some questions for reflection

- In what way is Jesus' teaching 'different' from that of the scribes, do you think? What would be the modern equivalent of these two styles of teaching?
- Does the Sermon on the Mount show something of the 'helplessness of God'?
- Does the life of Jesus offer a model for the exercise of leadership or authority within Christianity today?

CHAPTER NINE

Power and authority in Mark's Passion narrative (the helplessness of God)

We are still following the text of the Spiritual Exercises that have inevitably so powerfully affected Pope Francis and given him the very new way of exercising authority that seems to be his. Now we enter the third week, which is given over to Jesus' suffering and death, and functions as a way of checking the reality of the decision that the retreatant has made in the course of the second week. It may be useful for us to remember the 'preparatory prayer' that the retreatant is to make before each period of prayer, which is 'to ask for what I want: sadness, grief, and shame, because for my sins the Lord is going to his Passion' (Exx 193). So the mood in which the retreatant confirms their decision has nothing of arrogance about it, but a clear-eyed recognition of the likely consequences of opting to serve God.

In this chapter I shall be arguing that in Mark's Passion narrative Jesus has things done to him, rather than being the person in charge. In the following chapter we shall be reading John's Passion narrative, which presents us with a Jesus who is much more in control, but still presents us with the 'helplessness of God'. It may be helpful in this chapter to recall Pope Francis' words to the cardinals, immediately after his election: 'When we walk without the cross, when we build without the cross and when we proclaim Christ without the cross, we are not disciples of the Lord. We are worldly.' That 'walking with the cross' is, it seems, how we are supposed to exercise leadership and authority in the Church.

We shall simply go through the extraordinary story which is Mark's Passion narrative. The story starts with what we may call a 'Marcan sandwich'. If we look at 14:1, 2, where the 'chief priests and scribes' are determined to kill Jesus, we see that it runs easily into verse 10, where Judas approaches them with an offer to hand Jesus over. I suggest that Mark has inserted the episode of the anointing of Jesus' feet at Bethany into the narrative. Mark does this quite often – wrapping one story round another – so that the reader can use them both to go deeper into the meaning. A good example is the story of Jairus' daughter (5:21-4a, 35-43) which frames the story of the woman with the haemorrhage (5:24b-34). In its present setting, the story of the anointing gives us a clue as to how we are to read the story of Jesus' Passion. It is, if you like, the lens through which to read the tragic tale that follows.

The story starts with a woman, unexpectedly and rather shockingly, coming into the place where the men are dining.[40] She then anoints Jesus with some of the very best available oil, and she disposes of it generously since she breaks the alabaster jar in which the oil was contained, so there is no possibility of keeping any of it back. Her generous gesture is, quite clearly, anointing Jesus as Messiah ('she poured it over his head', verse 3). Then, however, Mark offers us two possible interpretations of what the gesture might mean. The first is that of 'some people' (verse 4), who were very angry at the waste and the woman's failure to give the money to the poor 'and they snorted at her'. Then, however, Jesus offers an alternative interpretation (verses 6-9). First he affirms that it has been a good thing to do and, implicitly, that recognising who Jesus is matters far more

---

40. Mark 14:3. This is a place where she has no business to be.

than even giving to the poor, because 'me you do not always have'. Then he reinterprets what the woman has done: it is not, as we had supposed when we read verse 3, simply anointing Jesus as Messiah, but also affirming what kind of Messiah Jesus is: 'she took the myrrh in advance to anoint my body for burial'. So Jesus is not just any kind of Messiah (for Mark), but a *dying* Messiah. We shall have to preserve the recollection of this story all the way through our reading of Mark's Passion story as we watch Jesus' intense vulnerability.

Not that Jesus is without authority in this Passion narrative, as we see in the next episode (14:12-25). The disciples, who almost always get things wrong in Mark's Gospel, show a degree of ineptitude when they come to ask Jesus, 'Where do you want us to prepare for you to eat the Passover?' We know that Jerusalem was always absolutely full (and tense) at Passover time, so it was, to be frank, a little bit slow of them only to have thought of it at this point. Then, however, we learn that Jesus has the whole thing under control, and indeed has already arranged a coded signal: 'Go into the city, and a man will meet you, carrying a pot of water. Follow him.' When I taught in Africa, my students immediately knew that something was odd here, for carrying jars of water is not done by men but by women and children. However, Jesus is in charge, and employs the discipleship word 'follow him'.

They settle down to eat the Passover meal, which should be a joyful occasion, with the youngest member of the community asking questions about what there is about 'this night' that makes it so special. Instead of that, however, 'as they lay down and ate' (14:18), Jesus makes his disconcerting solemn affirmation, utterly jarring in the context: 'Amen I am telling you, that one of you is going to hand me over – the one who is eating with me.' Not surprisingly, this causes immense distress, and they all start asking, 'It's not me, is it?' Jesus' response emphasises the terrible sadness of the situation, in the careful phrasing of 'one of the Twelve, the one who dips into the bowl with me'. This implies an appalling breach of Near Eastern hospitality codes, and also stresses the helplessness of Jesus in his work for God's project, handed over by one of the very people ('one of the Twelve') who have been selected and trained for that project. So it is not the case that God effortlessly conquers the world to his will.[41]

Then the darkness becomes obscurer yet with Jesus' next remark. For 'having taken bread, he blessed and broke and gave to them'. These words are so very familiar to us that we hardly notice them any more, but we should link them to what follows: 'This is my body.' However you understand that, clearly it carries more than a hint of death about it. This becomes clearer as he continues, repeating the same actions over the cup and pronouncing, after they have all drunk from it, in apparent explanation of what is going on, 'This is my blood of the covenant, which is poured out for many', and a slightly mysterious codicil, 'Amen I'm telling you, I shall never again drink of the fruit of the vine until that day when I drink it new in the Kingdom of God.' We are clearly approaching a decisive moment.

From the upper room, Jesus and the disciples proceed (after singing hymns) to the Mount of Olives, where Jesus makes some very authoritative predictions (14:26-31). Now to some extent, if you can predict you are in control, and so you might say Jesus is in charge. He is, however, still somewhat helpless, as he declares that 'you will all be made to stumble', and implies that he ('the shepherd' referred to in

---

41. Though the reader will notice the dark prediction of the betrayer's fate at the end of verse 21.

Zechariah 13:7) is going to be 'struck', and all the sheep 'scattered'. This is true even though he goes on to predict his resurrection (verse 28); the reader may care to reflect that resurrection implies the death that must come first.

There is little time for reflections of this sort, however, since Peter takes up the reference to being 'made to stumble' and is given a very solemn warning: 'Amen I am telling you that you, *today, on this very night*, before the cock has crowed twice, are three times going to deny me'. Peter is on a roll, however, and with more than a hint of posturing, 'started saying emphatically, "Even if I have to die with you, no way am I going to deny you". And they all said the same.' None of this inspires any confidence in the future of God's project.

The next thing to happen might encourage us, for now Jesus hands over authority to the Father, and is thereafter, surprisingly enough, in control (14:32-42). We notice once more that his disciples are not up to much, since they are told to 'sit here, while I pray', which suggests that they are not even up to that relatively undemanding activity. Then, along with the 'inner cabinet' of Peter, James and John, we are witness to immense stress on Jesus' part (Mark uses two verbs which mean something like 'alarmed' and 'distressed'). We eavesdrop as he talks first to his disciples ('My soul is deeply grieved, to the point of death; stay here, and keep awake'), and then to the God whom he calls 'Father', begging that 'the hour should pass from him, if possible'. Mark gives us precise words, even in Aramaic: 'Abba, Father, take this cup away from me,' with the all-important proviso, 'but not what I want, but what you want.' God's project does not appear to be in great shape just at present, and this is underlined by the fact that his elite group is fast asleep and has to be told, 'Stay awake, and pray not to come into temptation.' The mission is seriously flawed, and this is underlined when Jesus returns twice more to find them still sleeping 'for their eyes were weighed down – and they had no idea what to say to him'. Finally Jesus tells them, perhaps even with a touch of humour, 'Sleep now, and have a rest. It is enough: the hour has come. Look! The Son of Man is being handed over into the hands of sinners.' We may notice, perhaps, that Jesus is speaking here with a certain authority after his apparently despairing prayer.

The following section presents the arresting party (14:43-50) which, by contrast, requires secular support, namely weapons and a secret sign: 'The one whom I kiss, you are to arrest him, and lead him away securely.' It is true that 'one of the bystanders drew his sword and struck the High Priest's slave, and took off his ear lobe', but Mark's Jesus shows no sign of any interest in such extravagant gestures; instead he comments that they had never showed signs of wanting to arrest him when he was teaching in the Temple. He merely contents himself with saying, authoritatively enough, 'Let the Scriptures be fulfilled', which is, of course, one way of saying that God's project is working itself out in this apparent catastrophe.

We are made aware, however, of Jesus' helplessness: all of his companions who a few verses earlier were proclaiming that they were ready to die with Jesus now play a very different tune: 'They abandoned him and ran away – every single one of them.' Mark then underlines Jesus' lonely helplessness with an episode that is found in no other Gospel:

> And a certain young man was following with him, wearing a linen cloth over his naked body. And they arrest him. However he abandoned the linen cloth, and ran away naked.
>
> *Mark 14:51, 52*

Clearly we are meant to applaud the young man for 'following with' Jesus, for that is a discipleship word in Mark's Gospel. We may also be invited to sympathise with him, having to run away naked, for the naked body was not a cultural value in the Jewish world, and there is a real humiliation here. We notice, further, that he was wearing a *sindon* – a linen cloth. The next time we shall meet this word is in the following chapter (15:46), where such a garment is purchased and used to wrap Jesus' corpse before it is placed in the tomb. So there is clearly some connection between the disciple of Jesus who runs away and the dying Jesus who is not found in his tomb on the Sunday morning. For our purposes, however, it is perhaps enough to notice Jesus' utter loneliness and helplessness at this vital moment in the project of God.

In the next episode (14:53-65), it gets worse, for the next thing that happens is that Jesus is brought before the Sanhedrin – 'the High Priest, and all the high priests and the elders and the scribes'. The narrative then takes a break – another 'Marcan sandwich' – as Peter, still following a long way off, is put into position. Then we return to the Sanhedrin and learn that the agenda is not a juridical investigation so much as an attempt at murder: 'They started to look for evidence against Jesus, in order to put him to death – and they found none.' Just for a moment it seems that it may, after all, be the religious authorities who are engaged on a hopeless project, especially when the next set of (lying) witnesses cannot even make their stories match, as they claim that Jesus has announced, 'I'm going to destroy this Temple made by human hands, and build another, not made by human hands.'

The next step therefore is to get Jesus to condemn himself, and so the High Priest, irritated by Jesus' silence, 'stood up into the middle, and interrogated him and says to him: "Are you the Messiah, the son of the Blessed One?"' We must imagine a pause as this momentous question sinks in, and then, in a voice that echoes down the ages, Jesus responds, 'I AM . . . and you will see the Son of Man sitting on the right hand of power, and coming with the clouds of heaven', citing Daniel 7:13. This is, if you like, a declaration of power. It comes very close indeed to an affirmation of Jesus' divinity, but at the same time it precipitates Jesus' death. So helplessness is, once more, at the heart of the divine project.

The High Priest, by contrast, has an agenda (as we are already aware), and he is able to perform the theatrical gesture of tearing his clothes and delivering the verdict: 'What further need do we have of witnesses? You have heard the blasphemy! How does it look to you?' It is only in the last sentence that he actually goes through the formality of consulting the other legal experts. Then at last Jesus is sentenced to death, and spat upon and hooded and beaten and jeered at and slapped. At this point he seems utterly helpless, and is hardly exercising any kind of leadership at all.

Now things get worse (14:66-72). Peter, whom we last saw at 14:54 'following from a long way off', and therefore still a disciple, if rather a remote one, is now observed doing just what Jesus had predicted and absolutely denying that he has ever heard of Jesus. As with all the best stories, it comes in three parts. First he is observed 'warming himself' by one whom Mark describes, almost untranslatably, as 'just one woman, from the slavelings of the High Priest'. In such a culture that person is right at the bottom of the heap, but she has the courage to look at Peter and tell the truth: 'You were with the Nazarene, that Jesus.' In response to the truth, where his master had been silent in response to lies, Peter makes altogether too much noise: 'I have no idea, nor do I understand, what you are saying', and goes into retreat mode: 'He went out, outside, into the forecourt.' This brings him no respite, however, for 'the little slave-girl started saying to the bystanders, "He's one of *them*."' Peter is now locked into denial, but then the bystanders chime in, 'You are certainly one of them; because you are a Galilean.'[42] Peter is utterly trapped, and we listen in horror as he 'began to curse and swear, "I don't know this person whom you are talking about."' Then comes the moment that Jesus (not so helpless, after all?) predicted:

> And immediately, for a second time, the cock crowed; and Peter remembered the word, how Jesus had told him, 'Before the cock crows twice, you're going to deny me three times'. And he broke down and wept.
> *Mark 14:72*

With the skill of a consummate narrator, Mark leaves the story just there.

Now things get much more serious (15:1-15). Jesus is tied up and handed over to the local representative of the imperial power – Pontius Pilate – so he is utterly helpless. We notice, however, that he has sufficient self-possession to maintain his silence. Pilate asks him the dangerous question, 'Are you the King of the Jews?' Jesus merely replies laconically, 'You say so', and then lapses into silence in the face of the allegations of the religious establishment and Pilate's own interrogation. Mark comments, 'with the result that Pilate wondered'. It is Jesus who dominates this scene, even though it is Barabbas, not Jesus, whom the crowds are demanding. We observe that Pilate twice names Jesus as 'King of the

---

42. Matthew 26:73 is probably correct in suggesting that they spotted his impenetrable accent.

Jews' (verses 9, 12), whereas all the crowds will say of Jesus is, 'Crucify him!' In the end, therefore, Pilate flogs him and hands him over 'for him to be crucified'. It is an extraordinary scene, and it is not Pilate who catches the eye.

Then things become odder yet, as Jesus is mocked as a fake king (15:16-20). The soldiers put a purple (that is to say a royal or senatorial) robe on him in the presence of the entire cohort. They give him a crown, for kings need a crown, even if it is made out of thorns, and address him in the form appropriate for a monarch, 'All hail, Your Majesty of the Judeans!' Then there must be a sceptre of office and homage, but instead they 'hit him on the head with a reed, and spit on him and went down on their knees in homage to him'. And when the fun is over, they take off the purple robe and put Jesus' own clothes back on him, 'and they lead him out to crucify him'.

In 15:21-32, Jesus is glimpsed in one moment of independence when he is offered 'wine mixed with myrrh' – possibly a kindly offer of a narcotic to dull the pain – which he refuses. After that, he is utterly helpless, as 'they crucify him, divide his garments, casting lots over them [to see] who would have them'. The indignity is compounded when an inscription indicating the legal grounds of his execution is inscribed 'The King of the Judeans'. The mocking theme of royalty continues when 'two brigands' (just like Barabbas) are crucified on either side of Jesus; 'one on his right and one on his left' is clearly intended to remind us of the foolish request of James and John to join him in his glory (10:37). This appalling ending is the 'glory' to which God's helpless project has now come, in a parody of enthronement ceremonies. It gets worse, as the fawning flattery normally given to royalty is replaced with 'wagging of heads' and jeering on the part of passers-by, and the 'high priests' have their fun, suggesting that 'he "saved" others – he can't save himself! Let the Messiah, the "King of Israel" come down from the cross now! For us to see and believe!' Even his fellow convicts 'reviled him'.

And it seems that God is helpless to intervene, since, after six dreadful hours of this humiliating exposure, Mark allows us to hear Jesus bellow (in his native Aramaic), 'My God, my God – why have you abandoned me?' Even at that point Jesus is misunderstood, for the Aramaic word 'Elohi' ('my God') is misunderstood as 'Elijah', who might be coming to intervene to prevent disaster. Nothing of the sort happens, of course, and Jesus, quite unmistakably, dies on a loud shout (15:33-7).

Then, in two rather odd ways, Jesus is vindicated (15:38, 39), but somewhat unexpectedly. In the first place 'the veil of the Temple was cut [or 'divided'] in two, from top to bottom'. Quite clearly, this is to be understood as God's intervention, the divine comment on what has just happened, just as it had clearly been God who cut/divided the heavens at Jesus' baptism (1:10). Secondly, and equally unexpectedly, we overhear the verdict of 'the centurion [of all people!] who stood over against him' who comments, having seen Jesus die in this helpless way, 'Truly, this man was Son of God.'

We notice two ways in which Jesus is not, after all, completely alone. First, in 15:21, we are introduced to the African figure of Simon the Cyrenean, who is compelled to assist in the carrying of Jesus' cross (so it was not the fruit of a generous desire to assist this 'poor criminal'). However, it is clear that something happened to this stray caught up in the adventure, since Mark tells us that he is 'the father of Alexander and Rufus', which must mean that they are known to Mark's church, and suggests that on that Friday afternoon Simon saw the truth of what was going on and became a disciple of Jesus, along with his family.

Not only that, but Mark suddenly allows us to notice that the women are there, looking on from afar, among whom were:

> Mary the Magdalen, and Mary of Jacob the less, and the mother of Joses, and Salome; these women had been his disciples in Galilee and had served him – and there were many other women who had come up with him to Jerusalem.
>
> *Mark 15:40, 41*

This is, of course, a vindication, but they are only women (we hear the reader exclaim), so it does not make any difference, and God's project is still helpless in catastrophe.

The helplessness of the project is now made absolutely clear, as Jesus is buried (15:42-47). However, the burial story that Mark tells is rather odd. Firstly, and quite unexpectedly, the person responsible for the burial turns out, after all, to be someone of some standing – 'a prominent counsellor, who was also expecting the Kingdom of God' (as had been proclaimed by Jesus at the beginning of his mission, 1:14, 15). Not only that, but Joseph is in a position to enter into high-level negotiations with Pilate and with the centurion and to attain his objective: 'he bought a *sindon* [that word again] took him down, wrapped him in the *sindon*, and placed him in a tomb which was carved out of the rock, and rolled a stone at the door of the tomb.'

End of story, you might suppose, except that the women make a final appearance: 'Mary the Magdalen and Mary of Joses saw where he was put.' That, of course, is a hint, looking ahead at what is to follow, that God is not, after all, quite so helpless. But we are not there yet.

Conclusion

Mark, then, presents us with a Jesus who is utterly helpless in his Passion. There are hints, but we have to be watching for them, that God's project is not, after all, to be frustrated, but we are not reading the Gospel properly if we discount the awfulness of it.

Neither, returning once more to the theme of the Spiritual Exercises, must we avoid the reality check that Mark's reading of the Passion story offers to our decision about lifestyle that we may have made in an exuberant moment of enthusiasm. This chapter asks us: are you prepared to accept the cost?

Some questions for reflection

- Are you prepared to accept the cost?
- Is God's project utterly helpless?
- Who is really in charge here?

CHAPTER TEN

Power and authority in John's Passion narrative

In this chapter we shall continue our journey through the third week of the Spiritual Exercises, when Ignatius offers the retreatant a chance to check out their decision about lifestyle against the reality of its likely consequences, namely joining Jesus in his suffering and death. In this week of the Exercises we are invited to pray for the grace of experiencing the shame of the cross. You may feel that to be easy enough if the setting is the rather bleak one of Mark's Gospel. In this chapter we shall be reading through John's Passion narrative which, as we shall see, makes of the cross something of a royal throne. Nevertheless, it remains a cross, and a good way of confirming our election, or choice. It also, of course, gives us a clue about the way in which authority and power are to be managed in the Jesus movement.

It is helpful to start by reflecting on the setting that John gives his Passion narrative, which is extraordinarily different from the other three, not least because of the four chapters of the Last Supper Discourse (chapters 13-17). They begin with 'love' (see 13:1, where the verb appears twice) and end with love (see 17:24-6, where the noun appears once and the verb twice). Not only that, but these chapters start with a dramatised parable of love – the washing of the disciples' feet (13:1-20) – presented as an icon of how love is to be given expression in the Christian community. John places the episode precisely where his readers, brought up on Mark and the Synoptics, would have expected to find the institution of the Eucharist. What the evangelist is doing therefore is presenting the 'real significance' of Christian participation in the Eucharist: those who lead in the Jesus movement are to express their authority by performing the disgusting functions that are reserved for slaves. Not surprisingly, Simon Peter, who will later exercise a leadership function in the community, cannot cope with this ('No way are you going to wash my feet – ever!' 13:8), so Jesus explains that allowing oneself to be served by the leader is how you come to have a part in him. After that he applies the enacted parable to demonstrate how leadership is to be exercised in the Jesus movement:

> You address me as 'Teacher' and 'Lord' – and that is well said, because that is what I am. So if I have washed your feet (your 'Teacher' and 'Lord'), then you are to wash each other's feet.
>
> *Mark 13:13, 14*

This is quite a challenge, to which we in the Church have not always lived up.

There is not sufficient space here to work through the whole of the Last Supper Discourse (chapters 13–17), but if you want to get a feel of it, you could do worse than count the number of times the noun or verb 'love' appears in these chapters. You should especially notice one particular use of the word 'love' – Jesus' reference at 15:13 to 'greater love' and the fact that it consists in dying for others. That is certainly a model for leadership in the Church, and the reader is well aware that this discourse is put on to Jesus' lips precisely on the night before he died.

So when we read the Passion narrative in the fourth Gospel, the seed has already been sown for us to see it as an act of self-denying love.

The story starts in a garden (18:1), and we look ahead to Jesus' burial in a garden (19:41) and to the encounter of Mary Magdalen with one whom she assumes to be a passing gardener (20:15). It is not out of the question that we may also be invited to think of the most famous garden of all – that of 'Eden in the East' (Genesis 2:8) where the human story started, and where it began to go horribly wrong. So there may be a clue here that this Passion story is the restoration of humanity from the mess in which it finds itself.

One of the characteristics that we encounter immediately here is Jesus' authority. Look at how the narrative starts, with a contrast between what Judas knows, namely the place where Jesus tended to gather with his disciples (verse 2), and what Jesus knows, namely 'everything that was coming upon him' (verse 4). This 'knowledge' of Jesus stays with him to the very end, so that in 19:28 the evangelist indicates that 'Jesus knew that everything was accomplished'. The point is not that 'knowledge is power', as the bellicose cliché has it, but that true knowledge is a grasp of what is going on in God's project, in order the better to serve it.

The contrast between Judas and Jesus goes deeper in what happens next, for Judas' arresting party needs a whole array of useful contrivances to defend their project: a 'cohort' (18:3), then 'servants, lamps, torches, weapons', and (in verses 12, 24) 'chains'. Jesus, by contrast, has no implements at all, but is utterly in charge. It is he who leads the interrogation: 'Whom are you looking for?' (verse 4) and he who gives the orders: 'If it is I whom you are looking for, let these people go' (verse 8). Here we may contrast the earlier version of this question, back in 1:38 – '*What* are you looking for?' – the reader has to move from a 'what' to a 'who'.[43] In

---

43. And compare the question to Mary Magdalen in the garden in 20:15.

the end, the successful reader of John's Gospel is the one who accepts the invitation to go deeper into the mystery of who Jesus is. But it is perfectly possible to refuse the invitation, and so, once again, God's project is helplessly dependent upon human response.

We should pause to observe the effect of Jesus' self-designation. When he interrogates the arresting-party as to whom they are seeking and is told 'Jesus the Nazarene' (18:5), he responds, '*Ego Eimi*'. This could here be translated as 'That's me', but should be better understood as the ancient divine title of 'I AM'. This idea is frequently employed in this Gospel; in the present instance it is a saying of immense power, as we see when he employs this expression: 'They went away backwards, and fell to the ground' (verse 6). It is clearly a self-designation that carries considerable weight. At this stage, you may feel that any sense of the 'helplessness' of God's project is tendentious. Notice, however, if that is the way you are thinking, that Jesus at no point exercises his undoubted power in such a way as to evade the death that is coming upon him.

This becomes clearer if we compare Jesus' response with that of Simon Peter at the moment of the arrest (verses 10, 11): 'So Simon Peter, who had a sword, drew it, and struck the slave of the High Priest, and cut off his ear lobe, the right-hand one'. We are clearly not supposed to be impressed with this reaction: what possible help, after all, could the removal of an ear lobe, on whichever side, offer Jesus? It has to be admitted, of course, that Christians have all too often supposed that a violent response is the best way of dealing with aggression. Instead we should listen, it seems, to the approach of Jesus (who is almost weary at the absurdity): 'Put your sword back into its scabbard: am I not to drink the cup that the Father has given me?' There is real authority here, and the Jesus movement has been insufficiently attentive to the sound of it.

The same authority is detectable when the High Priest interrogates Jesus (18:19-24). Very calmly he responds to the cross-examination with a statement of the obvious:

> I have always spoken openly in synagogue and in the Temple, where all the Judeans gather; and I said nothing in secret. Why interrogate me? Instead you should interrogate those who heard what I said to them. Look – these people know what I said.
>
> *John 18:20, 21*

This elicits a violent response, such as authority, or its lower minions, is all too likely to offer: 'When he said this, one of the servants, who was standing by, gave Jesus a slap, saying, "Is that how you respond to the High Priest?"' We watch a little nervously to see whether this aggressive toady will be given the *Ego Eimi* treatment and be knocked to the ground, but that is not the way Jesus behaves. Instead he answers with devastating logic, and with profound authority: 'If I have spoken in an evil manner, give evidence about the evil. But if I have spoken well, why are you hitting me?' And we notice that the religious establishment is simply unable to cope any more, 'And so Annas sends him in chains to the High Priest Caiaphas', who immediately delivers him, like a hospital pass in rugby football, on to Pilate (18:28).

At this point the evangelist does something very interesting for our purposes, as we seek to see the way in which authority is appropriately exercised in the Jesus movement and the temptations that can afflict those in (especially religious) authority. The next thing that happens is that Jesus' trial continues on two stages, carefully set up by the author. If you look at 18:28, 33, 19:1 (though admittedly it is only implicit here), 19:9, 13, you will see that they are placed *inside* the praetorium, whereas the following verses are *outside*: 18:29, 38; 19:4, 5, 13. *Inside* we are eye-witnesses to a debate between Jesus and a Pilate who is rapidly losing his grip on the situation, and the subject of the debate is the nature of 'kingship'. *Outside* are those of the religious establishment who, we learn, are anxious not to defile themselves so that they might eat the Passover (18:28). On the other hand, though, they seem not especially troubled about certain irregular features of the situation. They are not worried about a formal trial, it appears (verse 30), and homicide is certainly on the agenda (verse 32). You may wish to reflect on parallels you have known, where those in power – even religious authorities – have placed their own narrow interests, or power games, ahead of the needs of the vulnerable and innocent.

This observation gives a certain sharpness to the debate that we witness going on inside the praetorium between Pilate and Jesus. As we have mentioned, the debate is all about kingship, and what it means to be a king, and whether Caesar (the Roman emperor currently reigning – in this case the melancholy emperor Tiberius) was really a king. There is also, of course, the question of whether Jesus is a king. In some sense, we already know from Nathanael's exuberant comment in 1:49 that there is a sense in which Jesus is indeed a king. This is modified to some extent when in 3:3 Jesus uses the Synoptic phrase 'the kingdom of *God*' in his conversation with Nicodemus. However, we notice that someone described as a 'royal official' (4:46, 49) is actually seen begging (and then obtaining) a favour from Jesus. We learn from his escape into the hills in 6:15 that he is not a king in any ordinary sense. However, when Jesus enters Jerusalem (12:13-15), he is twice referred to as 'King of Israel' and as 'your king' without any reservation on the part of the evangelist. He is a king of some kind.

All this is part of the background of our passage, 18:33–19:21, where the reader is presented with a *concentration of texts* about kingship and authority. It starts with Pilate (in a very odd question) demanding to know if Jesus is the King of the Judeans. Jesus responds in terms that make it sound like an intellectual debate: 'Is it on your own account that you say this, or did other people tell you about me?' Pilate tries to avoid getting drawn in: 'Am I a Judean? It is your race, and your high priests who have handed you over to me.' Then comes another very odd question, considering the circumstances: 'What have you done?' The answer to this is presumably Pilate's job to discover, not the task of the accused to tell him. Pilate is, however, not up to the challenge and cannot compete with Jesus for moral stature, as the Galilean criminal goes on:

> My kingdom is not from this world; if my kingdom were from this world, my servants would have struggled to prevent me being handed over to the Judeans. As it is, my kingdom is not from this world.

The one who makes these remarks is walking in a place where Pilate cannot go, as he despairingly asks, 'So you are a king, then?' (or, just possibly, 'So you are not a king, are you?'). And Jesus once again moves in a more rarefied atmosphere as he continues:

> It is you who are saying that I am a king. It was born for this, and for this I have come into the world, that I might bear witness to the truth. Everyone who is from the truth listens to my voice.

All Pilate can manage is the evasive, 'What is truth?' He rushes out and tries to pronounce Jesus Not Guilty, then offers to release 'the King of the Judeans' as a Passover present. However, they all bellow for 'Barabbas', and the evangelist laconically comments that 'Barabbas was a brigand' (18:40).

The next step is for Jesus to be flogged, by way of preparation for crucifixion, which is hardly typical treatment for a king. The soldiers now engage in a ghastly parody of enthronement, with a crown and a purple garment and acclamations of 'Hail, King of the Judeans!' and slaps (once more) instead of sycophantic gestures of homage.

Somehow, though, it does not quite work, since the next time we see Jesus, 'He came out, outside, wearing the crown of thorns and the purple cloak, and [Pilate] said, "Look! The man."' Jesus is very much in charge; this scene gives him immense authority, and Pilate, almost despite himself, is bearing witness to his stature. The Judean religious establishment, however, will have none of it, and repeat their demand for blood (19:6, 7).

So Pilate goes back inside (19:8, 9) and asks his first intelligent question: 'Where are you from?' Jesus, however, says nothing, and his silence is regal. This is backed up when Pilate, with just a touch of petulance, like a teacher who feels that he has lost his control of the class, asks, 'Are you not talking to me? Don't you realise that I have authority to set you free, and I also have authority to crucify you?' Jesus takes up that keyword and throws it back at the Roman Emperor's local representative: 'You would have absolutely no authority against me unless it had been given you from above. Therefore the one who handed me over to you has the greater sin' (verse 11). Pilate is dismissed as a relatively unimportant sinner.

Now Pilate tries once more to let Jesus off and is firmly told, 'If you let this one off, you are not a friend of Caesar. Everyone who makes himself a king is contradicting Caesar' (19:12). That, of course, is the one thing that Pilate cannot afford, and he does not have the moral authority to stand up for himself against the crowd.

We may notice, as we go through this story, that at no stage has Jesus attempted to make himself king; royal emanations just come out of him. This becomes absolutely pellucid when he comes to judgement at Lithostrotos: you cannot tell from the Greek whether it is Pilate or Jesus who is sitting in judgement, and to our astonishment (and possibly to Pilate's also) we hear the Roman Governor proclaiming, 'Look – your king!' (19:14). He tries to shout down their demands for blood – 'Is it your king whom you want me to crucify?' – which only elicits from them the terrible verdict, denying the entire history of the people of God, 'We have no king but Caesar!'

That is the end of the debate, but not of the manifestation of Jesus' authority. Now he is seen 'carrying the cross for himself' (19:17). John's Jesus has no need of Simon of Cyrene, even if he is now crucified and therefore finally helpless. Still, however, the theme of kingship is played, for the evangelist says that 'Pilate wrote an inscription and placed it on the cross; and it was written "Jesus the Nazarene, the King of the Judeans".' We further learn that it was written in the three principal languages that might be used thereabouts, namely Aramaic, Latin and Greek, and that the Judean authorities wanted to alter it from affirming Jesus' kingship to indicating simply that 'He said, "I am King of the Judeans"' (19:21), which we know not to have been the case. Pilate has now had enough, and sends them packing with, 'What I have written I have written' (verse 22).

It is a remarkable picture, and we are not permitted to evade the question of whether or not Jesus was a king. He is a king of a very different kind, and not one who may be expected to exercise his authority in any very powerful way. He is, for one thing, on the point of a horrible and humiliating death. The evangelist, however, is in no doubt that this is all 'God's project', and one of the ways in which he makes this point is by way of his insistence that the Scriptures are fulfilled: 19:24, 28, 36-7. And oddest of all is that at 18:32 it is not the Scriptures that are fulfilled but Jesus' own words, which have taken on a very lofty status.[44]

Perhaps most royal of all is what happens at the end, when Jesus, on the point of death, founds a dynasty. The evangelist draws our attention quite suddenly to the presence of his mother, and then to that of the Beloved Disciple, whose appearance takes us very much by surprise. To them he says, first, 'Woman – look: your son', and then to the disciple, 'Look – your mother'. The evangelist then comments that 'from that hour the disciple took her to his own' (19:25-27). This echoes what he had said in the prologue, that Jesus 'came to his own, and his own did not receive him' (1:11).

So Jesus, at the end of the Passion narrative of John's Gospel, is endowed with a certain unmistakable authority, as when he comes out 'wearing the crown of thorns and the purple garment', and with no sign of Simon of Cyrene,[45] 'carrying his cross for himself' (19:5, 17), as we have seen. This authority is at its clearest just before Jesus dies. So in 19:28 we read, 'After this, Jesus *knowing* [that word again, cf. 18:4] that already everything had been accomplished, in

---

44. We might perhaps compare 2:22, where we are told that after the resurrection the disciples 'believed the Scripture and the word that Jesus had spoken' after the incident in the Temple.
45. For whom, as we have seen, the Fourth Gospel has no place.

order that the Scriptures might be fulfilled, said, "I thirst."' The point here is that Jesus is very much in charge, that he has 'knowledge', and that he is engaged on God's project. It is true that he is thirsty, and in contrast to the episode at the well with the Samaritan woman in chapter 4, this time he is actually given a drink; but the point for the evangelist seems mainly to be that Jesus is here fulfilling Psalm 22:15.

This leads straight in to the account of Jesus' death (19:30): 'When he had accepted the vinegar, Jesus said "It is accomplished" and bowing his head, handed over the Spirit.' Once more, we see a Jesus who is very much in charge: he accepts the vinegar as a gift, he pronounces that God's project 'has been fulfilled', then, in an act of gracious acceptance, he bows his head, accepting death. The final line could be translated as 'he gave up the ghost' – that is to say, simply, that 'he died'. It is also, however, for John's Gospel, the moment of the gift of the Spirit,[46] so we equally translate it as 'he handed over the Spirit'.

There are two more details of this Passion narrative that might be classed as royal. The first is related in the following terms:

> One of the soldiers pierced his side with a lance – and immediately there came out blood and water. And the one who saw it has born witness, and his witness is true, and that person knows that he is telling true things, that you also may believe.
>
> *John 19:34, 35*

What is going on here? It is often understood as a reference to the Eucharist and to baptism, which may very well be the case: Jesus' death is seen as an authoritative gift of the

---

46. Cf. 7:39, where the evangelist comments that we cannot have the Spirit until Jesus is glorified; and of course 'glorification' in the fourth Gospel refers to Jesus' death, or 'lifting-up'.

sacraments. It may also refer to the promised gift of 'living water' that was referred to in Jesus' dialogue with the Samaritan woman (4:14, 15). Either way, it has to do with the gift that is Jesus' death.

The second royal detail of the narrative is Jesus' burial (19:38-42). As in Mark's Gospel, 'Joseph from Arimathea' asks Pilate for Jesus' body; this man is described as a secret disciple of Jesus. Pilate grants permission, then Nicodemus resurfaces from chapter 3,[47] bringing 'a mixture of myrrh and aloes, about a hundred litres', which is a spectacular quantity. These two then 'took the body of Jesus and wrapped it in cloths with spices (as is the burial custom for Judeans)'. Then we watch as the burial takes place, in 'a garden; and in the garden a new tomb in which no one had yet been laid. So there, because of the Preparation Day of the Judeans, because the tomb was nearby, they laid Jesus.' The solemnity of this 'state funeral' is unmistakable.

What, then, of the 'helplessness of God', of which we have been making so much? If the cross is really a royal throne on which Jesus is 'lifted up' and 'glorified', then is it not an exercise of power? To argue in this way is to miss the point. For one thing, Jesus is unmistakably dead. Resurrection has not yet happened, even though we think it may be on the way. For another thing, although Jesus has been revealed as authoritative and very much in charge during this Passion narrative, the last line has him, just as in Mark's Gospel, helplessly at the mercy of others: 'they laid Jesus'. Here he has absolutely no authority.

To conclude, therefore, the passion of Jesus, as John tells it, does have a regal aspect to it. However, by the end Jesus is

---

47. And cf. also 7:50, where he speaks up for Jesus.

a corpse, and (to revert to our consideration of the Spiritual Exercises) that corpse asks us if we are serious in the life choice that we made back in the second week. Triumph may indeed be on the way, but it has not yet happened, and we are faced with the question: are you prepared for the cost? If the question is put in this way, then there can be no possibility at all of our regarding discipleship as an opportunity for power games and evading the challenge of God's helplessness. Leadership in the Jesus movement is not a matter of power.

Some questions for reflection
- In what ways does the Passion of Jesus help you to confirm your chosen vocation?
- Does the Passion narrative in Mark's Gospel have anything to say about how authority should be exercised in the Church today?
- John's Gospel presents Jesus' cross as a 'royal throne'. Does that offer a different angle on the question of 'authority'?

CHAPTER ELEVEN

Power and authority in the resurrection

So at last we come to the fourth week of the Spiritual Exercises, at which we have been aiming all this time. In this chapter I should like to argue three things:

1. that resurrection changes everything
2. that resurrection is at the heart of our faith
3. that resurrection gives us a job to do.

It is the mood in which we should leave retreat. So we take note of the prayer that we are to make in the fourth week, 'to ask for the grace to be glad and to feel intense joy at the great glory and joy that is Christ our Lord's' (Exx 221).

1. Resurrection changes everything

We have been on a long journey, first through what we call the 'Old Testament' and the encounter with our own sinfulness – roughly the first week of the Spiritual Exercises. Then we have moved into the second week, following Jesus' ministry as far as Palm Sunday. During that week the retreatant is invited to make a decision or choice of lifestyle. The third week invited us to pray Jesus' Passion, as a way of applying a reality test to that decision and asking for 'sadness, grief and shame'. Finally the fourth week offers joyful confirmation of the decision.

In their very different ways, each of the 27 books of the New Testament chronicles an explosion of theological activity arising out of the fact of Jesus' resurrection. Rather to their surprise, it seems, his first followers discovered, a couple of days after his appalling death, that Jesus had after all been vindicated by God. This, of course, changed everything, and meant that his followers needed to find an appropriate language in which to talk about him. Somehow or other the cross, which had seemed like the final defeat of God's all-too-vulnerable project, was after all the means of victory. And if God had raised Jesus from the dead (which no New Testament author ever doubts for a second) then Jesus was after all God's Messiah. They also found themselves driven, reluctantly – for they were good Jews – to use language to capture the reality of Jesus that had been hitherto reserved for God alone.

Here are some texts to show the difference that resurrection made. The first one is Mark 16:5, 6, which has the mysterious 'young man, sitting on the right, clothed in a white garment' who shows precise knowledge of the situation. In response to their great astonishment, he says, 'Don't be astonished. It is Jesus whom you are looking for, the Nazarene, the crucified one. He is risen; he is not here. Look! The place where they put him.' What the women were looking for was a corpse on whom they could lavish their last affections, with spices to anoint him (16:1). Clearly, therefore, they did not believe in resurrection, for in order to anoint a body it is required that it stay where it was last put. These brave women have no idea what has happened, nor did they have any expectation that it would happen. But what has happened – the absence of Jesus' body – has changed everything.[48]

---

48. Except, we have always to insist, the broad lines of the faithfulness of God, in the old story of God's people. The resurrection vindicates that story, remarkably and unexpectedly.

Matthew expresses the change in a rather different way:

And look! There was a great shaking;
for the angel of the Lord came down from heaven and approached
and rolled away the stone and sat on it.
And his appearance was like lightning, and his clothing white as snow.
From fear of him the watchers were shaken and became like corpses.
Matthew 28:2-4

Clearly everything has changed now. The 'shaking' is a symbol of this change, which happens both in general[49] and in particular, as the arrival of the 'angel of the Lord' reminds us of those dreams at the beginning of the Gospel.[50] The beginning and the end of the Gospel both assert that God is in charge, splendidly demonstrated by the angel first rolling the stone away and then sitting firmly on it. His attire, too, represents the presence of God.[51] 'Watchers' have been posted at the behest of the 'High Priests and Pharisees' (the religious authorities, that is to say), and with the acquiescence of Pilate (the supreme political authority), precisely to prevent any suggestion that 'he has been raised from the dead' on the 'third day' (27:62-6).

God's apparent helplessness turns out to be immense power, and those who are helpless are, oddly enough, the political and religious establishment. They demonstrate this, paradoxically enough, by bribing the guards who have reported the events to 'the high priests' and 'elders' to make the claim that the disciples 'came by night and stole the body' (28:11-13). Matthew notes (verse 15) that this is the

---

49. Possibly echoing the 'shaking' associated with resurrection from the dead, which had taken place at the moment of Jesus' death – 27:51, 52.
50. Matthew 1:20; 2:13, 19, 22.
51. The elements of 'lightning' and 'white as snow'.

story that is circulating today among the Jews. In terms of the Spiritual Exercises, we are asked to 'be glad and feel intense joy', which is as it should be, at this complete change in the course of events.

Our next text is Luke 24:3-8, which gives much the same information as we see in Mark. It starts with the women 'scratching their heads' over the absence of 'the body of the Lord Jesus'. They then encounter not one but two men who, as in Mark, are wearing 'clothing that flashes like lightning'. The women clearly experience this as a numinous appearance,[52] since they 'became exceedingly afraid, and bowed their faces to the ground'. They are mildly reproached for not believing in resurrection: 'Why are you seeking the Living One with the corpses? He is not here – no, he is risen!' Then they are reminded about Jesus' teaching, 'how he told you while he was still in the Galilee . . . that the Son of Man necessarily . . . had to rise on the third day'. And then the women get it ('they remembered his words' – Luke 24:8).

So it was always going to happen, this resurrection, and in Luke's view they should have believed it, because God is in charge. But how do you grow into faith that this helpless God of ours is really able to deliver? Luke's solution is to use a word that could be translated as 'it is necessary'[53] or 'it was inevitable'.

We can see this in the next text that we have to consider – the lovely story of the journey to Emmaus (24:13-35). Luke has set this up as a liturgy, with a long penitential rite (verses 13-24) and then a liturgy of the word (sermon and biblical texts intermingled – 25-27). This is followed by the bidding prayers or prayers of intercession ('Stay with us' – verse 28),

---

52. So God is once more at work, even if obscurely.
53. In our translation of this passage it comes out as 'necessarily . . . had to rise'.

the Eucharistic liturgy (verses 30, 31), the reflection after communion (verse 32), and finally the dismissal (verses 33-5). We discover that Emmaus and Jerusalem are not nearly as far apart as we had supposed, that the Church knows (now) about resurrection, and that all experiences of the risen Christ can be shared. Everything has changed in this liturgy. We should notice, though, that the heart of the teaching is that 'it was necessary/inevitable that the Messiah should suffer and enter into his glory' (verse 26). This changes everything, while locating the outcome firmly in the context of the Old Testament story of God and the people of God.

Finally, in 24:36-48, Jesus' final encounter with the Church repeats the message. Quite suddenly, 'he himself stood in the midst of them and says to them, "Peace to you all."' You might expect, after all that has gone before, that they would say, 'Ah! There you are, Lord', since they believed that he was indeed raised from the dead; but not a bit of it. Instead, 'they became fearful, and thought that they were seeing a ghost'. So Jesus is required to demonstrate to them all over again that it really is he, and invites them to 'see my hands and my feet', to touch him and verify that he has 'flesh and bones'. When they still fail to believe ('from joy' as Luke charitably remarks), he eats a portion of grilled fish before their astonished gaze. The sheer ordinariness of the evidence that he gives underlines, as nothing else could, the nature of the change that has taken place. Everything is now different. And, once again (verse 44) the evangelist uses the word that means 'it is necessary/inevitable' with regard to the Messiah's suffering and resurrection.

So, finally, to John's Gospel, to see how the resurrection changes everything. We start with John 20:1-10. Mary, apparently unaccompanied (although in verse 2 she speaks of 'we'), runs to Peter and the Beloved Disciple, who in their turn 'run' to the tomb and enter, though not in the order of their arrival, and come to faith, 'for they did not yet know the Scripture that he had to rise from the dead'.

Perhaps the most dramatic account of how everything has changed comes in the verses that immediately follow (20:11-18) – a story that is all too rarely read in the liturgy. The focus returns once more to Mary (Magdalen) who is 'outside, weeping'. Nothing has yet changed in her life, even when she sees 'two angels, sitting in white things'. At first it appears that the corpse may be still there, for the narrator tells us that they were 'one at the head and one at the feet', but then he goes on, 'where the body of Jesus had lain'. Not unkindly, they ask her, 'Woman, why are you weeping?' to which she responds, 'They have taken away my Lord – and I don't know where they have put him.' In the awfulness, she does not pause to puzzle about the presence of angels or what it might mean, or even who they might be, but she turns away 'and sees Jesus standing there'. Since, however, nothing has changed as yet, she supposes him to be a passing gardener and she interrogates him about the missing corpse, with a view to giving it a proper burial.

Then we contemplate the moment when it all changes, and her interlocutor addresses her by name, 'Mariam', at which point she responds in their shared language of Aramaic, 'Rabbouni'. The unrecognised male, thought to be a gardener, though addressed accurately enough as 'Lord' (verse 15) is the one for whom she was longing. And it is now all different: she is told that she cannot continue to touch him since he has to 'ascend to the Father', but it really does not matter, because in that moment of recognition everything has changed.

The same thing happens again a few verses later, 'on the evening of that day' (verses 19-23), when the fearful disciples encounter him and he gives them the beautiful greeting, 'Peace to you' and provides evidence in the form of his wounded hands and side.[54] Then we have the Thomas story – another instance of how resurrection changes everything. Read this remarkable anecdote (20:24-9) and see how Thomas moves from a brutal and crude denial of the possibility of resurrection ('unless I see in his hands the mark of the nails, and unless I thrust my finger into the mark of the nails and unless I thrust my hand into his side, no way am I going to believe') to the astonishing statement, which goes way beyond the evidence, 'My Lord and my God'. The resurrection means that everything has changed. God may be helpless, but God's project will ultimately be victorious and, like Thomas, we shall come to recognise the truth about Jesus.

The final example of 'all change' is in chapter 21 of the fourth Gospel. It starts with 'everything is still just the same', as Simon Peter and six other disciples decide that they are going fishing, returning to their old profession. At first they are unsuccessful, until the shadowy figure of Jesus appears on the shore of the Sea of Tiberias and instructs them where to place their nets. The inevitable happens, and the nets are on the point of breaking. At that point, all changes, as the Beloved Disciple recognises that 'it is the Lord' (verse 7), which provokes Simon Peter to some inept behaviour – putting his clothes on in order to dive into the sea. Then we discover that they were only a hundred yards or so from the shore, so he could have got there by boat! Breakfast follows (verse 12), along with some apparent uncertainty about whom

---

54. So the evangelist implies that they did not believe what they saw.

they are dealing with ('they knew it was the Lord'), so that has not changed.

What happens next introduces a very radical change, as Peter is submitted to the three-fold interrogation about whether or not he loves Jesus (verses 15-19). Quite clearly this echoes his three-fold denial of Jesus on the Thursday evening. This reminder of his failure becomes the basis for asking him whether or not he loves Jesus, and then, as we shall shortly see, a platform for giving him a job to do. This is followed by a prediction of the unpleasant death that he is to suffer, after which he is told 'Follow me', and the reader is left to assume that Peter does indeed accept the invitation.

Everything is changed by resurrection, including what is to happen to the Beloved Disciple, in the episode that immediately follows (verses 20-3).

2. Resurrection is the heart of our faith: 1 Corinthians 15:1-8

For Paul, there is no Christianity without resurrection. The idea comes bubbling out from practically every line of his letters and is given dramatic expression by Luke on no less than three occasions.[55] Once Paul realised that he had met Jesus and that therefore the Christian claim about God having raised him from the dead was not crazy babbling but sober truth, the resurrection became the centrepiece of his entire life, and Paul fell in love with Jesus. We could pick a number of passages to illustrate this, but perhaps the best is the one that comes at the climax of his first letter to those squabbling Corinthian Christians. The difficulty that he is tackling here is that some in Corinth have been (as far as we can tell) asserting that, while Jesus may have been raised

---
55. Acts 9:1-19; 22:1-16; 26:12-23.

from the dead, those of their community who have died since Paul first preached the gospel to them have no access to resurrection (1 Corinthians 15:12-19). So, very patiently, he reminds them of the heart of his gospel:

> I'm making known to you, brothers and sisters, the gospel that I gospelled you,
> which you received, upon which you take your stand, through which you are being saved,
> in what terms I gospelled you (if you are holding it fast),
> *unless* you believed in vain.
> For I handed down to you in the first place, that which I also received, that Christ
> - *died* for our sins in accordance with the Scriptures, and that
> - *he was buried*, and that
> - *he was raised* on the third day in accordance with the Scriptures, and that
> - *he appeared* to Peter
> - and then to the Twelve.
> - Then *he appeared* to more than five hundred brothers and sisters all at once (the majority of whom remain to this day, though some have fallen asleep).
> - Then *he appeared* to James,
> - then to all the apostles.
> - Last of all, as though to an abortion, *he appeared* also to me. (You see, I am the least of the apostles; I'm not fit to be called an apostle, because I persecuted the church of God.) But by the grace of God I am what I am, and his grace in my regard has not been ineffective. No – I worked harder than all of them, or rather not I, but the grace of God that is with me.
>
> So – whether it's me or them, that is how we preach, and that is how you came to faith.
>
> *1 Corinthians 15:1-8*

Notice what Paul is doing here: he is reminding them of the basis of the gospel that they had accepted in Corinth (and elsewhere in the Mediterranean world) – namely that God had raised Jesus from the dead. He uses two verbs for 'tradition' from Jewish discourse – 'received', and 'handed down'; and one from Christian discourse[56] – namely 'gospel' and its cognate verb which I have translated, somewhat awkwardly, as 'gospelled'. Then Paul raises the question of whether or not the Corinthians have 'received' what he handed down to them: 'if you are holding it fast, *unless* you believed in vain' – which, knowing them, they may well have done. He sets the gospel out in terms of four verbs[57] – 'died', 'was buried', 'was raised', and 'appeared' – along with an impressive list of those by whom the risen Jesus 'was seen' (an alternative translation of the word rendered as 'appeared') – namely Peter, the Twelve, then 'five hundred brothers and sisters', 'all the apostles' (who are presumably a different set of people), and finally Paul himself.[58] Paul is absolutely clear that he has seen Jesus (cf. 1 Corinthians 9:1), even though he is 'not fit to be called an apostle', although the reader should be warned that while it is permissible for Paul to say this, when you meet him you should not say it to his face. The point, however, is clear: for Paul (and, I have to say, for all those early Christians), resurrection is at the heart of the gospel.

3. Resurrection gives us a mission/job to do

Not only that, but if it is true about resurrection, then we have a job to do. For evidence of that, we only need to look

---

56. Though it has a Jewish background.
57. Printed in italics in the extract above.
58. With whom the Corinthians will dispute at their peril.

at the life of St Paul after he met Jesus – how he rushed urgently round the Mediterranean world, preaching wherever he found himself in the big cities. Here we shall simply point to texts from the five Gospels.[59]

The first is Mark 16:7. After he has given them the Easter proclamation, 'He is risen, he is not here', the mysterious young man tells the women, 'But go and tell his disciples – and Peter – that he is going before you into the Galilee. There you will see him, as he told you.' The text leaves unresolved, however, the question of whether the women did what they had been told, since the Gospel originally ended, 'And the women went out and fled from the tomb, for trembling and amazement had seized them. And they said nothing to nobody. For they were afraid . . .' However, the reader will conclude that they must have said something to somebody, otherwise we would not be listening to the story. So there is a job to be done because of resurrection, but it is not an easy one.

The next text is from the additions to Mark that we find in Matthew's Gospel. At 28:7-10 we read his version of the preceding text. This is a rather different telling of the story, where the women 'came out quickly from the tomb, with fear and great joy, and ran to give the message to his disciples'. Their good intentions are then reinforced by an encounter with the risen Jesus himself:

> And look! Jesus met them, saying 'Rejoice'. And they approached and grabbed his feet; and they worshipped him. Then Jesus says to them, 'Don't be afraid. Off you go, and give the message to my brothers that they are to go into the Galilee – and they'll see me there.'

---

59. Counting Acts of the Apostles as a gospel of a sort.

So the repetition of the instructions gives the mission a certain solemnity.

Our next text is the closing words of Matthew's Gospel (28:16-20). This time it is the 'Eleven' who have a job to do. That number, which, as the reader is well aware, should be twelve,[60] has been broken by human sinfulness. This remnant obediently goes to the mountain ordained by Jesus, and Matthew comments that 'they worshipped him, but they doubted' (it is only fair to the reader to acknowledge that the second clause could be translated as 'but *some* doubted', although for our purpose it does not make much difference). Then they hear their mission. First there is an important preface: 'All authority has been given me [and the first-century hearer of these words would not need to be told that we are talking about God here as the source of the mission] in heaven and on earth.' Then the job description:

> Go and make disciples of all the Gentiles, baptising them into the name of the Father and of the Son and of the Holy Spirit, teaching them to keep all the things which I have commanded you.

The Gospel ends then with the indispensable condition for their doing the job: 'Look! I am with you all the days, until the consummation of the age'. That, you see, is what resurrection means.

Next we go to Luke and the lovely Emmaus story (24:13-35) which, as we have said, is a kind of liturgy. Like any good liturgy, the test of it is what it leads the participants to do. And in verses 33-5 the two people who have poured out their sadness to Jesus – not knowing that it was indeed the risen Jesus whom they were addressing – and then had their

---

60. Cf. Matthew 19:28.

'hearts burning' as he read the word to them and explained the text, find themselves covering the (hitherto impossibly long) journey back to Jerusalem to proclaim the good news. They have responded to the implicit *Ite Missa Est*[61] with which the liturgy ends, inviting the congregation's robust enthusiasm to be with the Church and to proclaim the resurrection.

The same effect is perceptible later in the same chapter (verses 47, 48), where Jesus appears 'in the midst of them' (verse 36) and explains that 'repentance for the forgiveness of sins is to be preached in his name to all the nations, beginning from Jerusalem'. And he ends with the direct command, 'You are witnesses to these things.' They cannot do it unaided, of course, and so they are told, 'I am sending the Promise of my Father upon you. You are to sit in the city until you are clothed with power from on high'.

The helplessness of God disappears with the resurrection, it seems, and instead we see the helplessness of the witnesses of the resurrection, who can only do their job with the help of the Holy Spirit. This theme continues into Luke's second volume, which can be read as an account of the Spirit driving these very human disciples to do their job. Look at Acts 1:8: immediately before the resurrection appearances come to an end with the Ascension, Jesus tells them:

> You are going to receive power when the Holy Spirit comes upon you; and you are going to be my witnesses in both Jerusalem and the whole of Judea, and in Samaria, and as far as the end of the earth.

---

61. The Latin dismissal at the end of mass, which is very hard to translate. 'Go, there is a sending' is a possible guess, or 'The mass is ended, go in peace' is a common modern attempt at it.

Once again the promise of the Holy Spirit is given, to compensate for the helplessness of the disciples. There is, however, a bit more to it this time, although, as before, they have the job of witnessing to do. This is to take place initially in the Holy Land, partly repeating the journey of Jesus from Galilee which took him through Samaria and Judea and ended in Jerusalem. Then, however, Acts takes a different turn, and the journey goes beyond Galilee to Athens (chapter 17) and finally ends in Rome (chapter 28). For Luke's purposes, these two destinations count as 'the end of the earth'.

The same task is enjoined in Acts 1:21, 22, in the context of the selection of a successor to Judas (to turn 'Eleven' back into 'Twelve'). Peter makes a speech to the group and indicates that the replacement has to be:

> one of the men who came with us in all the time when the Lord Jesus came in and went out upon us, beginning from the baptism of John until the day when he was taken up from us, a witness with us of his resurrection, to become one of these.

Once again, the job requires taking on the mission of being a witness to Jesus' resurrection.[62]

In the fourth Gospel, likewise, resurrection appearances reveal that there is a job to be done. At John 20:17, Mary is told, once she has recognised the gardener for who he is, 'Go to my brothers and sisters, and tell them, "I am going up to my Father, and to your [plural] Father, to my God and to your [plural] God."' And, we learn in verse 18 that Mary did precisely that. Likewise in 20:21-3, the disciples, locked in by their fear, are told, again once they have recognised who it

---

62. Interestingly, after they have prayed about it, Matthias is appointed by lot – and is never heard of again.

is, 'Peace be with you: as the Father has sent me, so I also send you.' Once again there is the gift of the Spirit, to cope with their helplessness, and the mission is made a bit more specific: 'Those whose sins you let go, they are let go; and those whose sins you hold fast, they are held fast'. Once more, we observe, God puts himself into the hands of those whom he sends; the helplessness of God should be a model for his disciples.

Finally, in chapter 21, Peter, as he is brought to face his own triple denial of Jesus, is given a job to do. After each of three protestations of his love he is told, 'Feed my lambs . . . Shepherd my sheep . . . Feed my sheep' (verses 15-17).

Conclusion

Our task therefore is clear: it is to proclaim the resurrection gospel and to look after those who are classified as Jesus' lambs and sheep. If we feel strongly that we are helpless to do such a thing, then there is the promise of the Holy Spirit. All this, however, can take place only once God's helplessness has been fully revealed. Anyone who thinks that leadership in the Jesus movement is a matter of power has not been reading the Gospels; authority in the Church has to do with testifying to the resurrection and modelling oneself on the helplessness of God.

A question for reflection

- Do you think it is true to say that the resurrection reveals the 'helplessness of God'? If so, how?

CHAPTER TWELVE

The Holy Spirit

In this chapter I should like to argue that the helplessness of God for which we have been arguing throughout this book is slightly deceptive. God is the creator of the universe, and exercises immense power. God is, however, voluntarily dependent on the loving response of the human race to whom he has given the dangerous gift of freedom. We used this freedom to bring about Jesus' death, and at that time only God's helplessness was apparent. Then Jesus was raised from the dead. Now that we have done our worst, it turns out that God has, after all, some power, but this power is not exercised in the way that we human beings naturally adopt. The source of all power is the Holy Spirit; the Holy Spirit is the 'climate' in which we should emerge from retreat, and so comes very appropriately at the end of our consideration of the Spiritual Exercises.

The prayer that the retreatant is encouraged to make in the course of this week is taken from Exercise 229, where we are 'deliberately wanting to be moved and to rejoice in the great joy and gladness of Christ our Lord'. There is no space here to offer a treatise on the Spirit in the New Testament; instead I offer just a few texts to encourage our prayer for the gift of the Spirit.

Inevitably we start with the end of Luke's Gospel and the beginning of Acts – the Gospel's second volume, which we shall be looking at both here and in Part III. The place to start is Luke 24:48, 49 and its dramatic realisation in the account of that first Pentecost – Acts 2:1-13. In the first of these texts, where Jesus sums up the whole of Luke's Gospel, the disciples are (as we saw in the previous chapter) told, 'You are witnesses of these things. And look! I am sending the promise of my Father upon you. You are to sit in the city, until you are clothed with power from on high.' That is clearly the gift of the Spirit for which we are to pray at this stage of the retreat.

Then we should read Luke's highly dramatic account of the coming of that gift (Acts 2:1-13). It starts with a characteristic Lucan expression: 'When the day of Pentecost was fulfilled'; that term 'fulfilled' indicates that God is in charge. Then we see the Church doing what the Church should do, namely being 'together in the same place'.[63] Then Luke gives dramatic expression to the coming of the Holy Spirit, first by a noise: 'Suddenly the sound from heaven as of a powerful wind being borne along', and then by a sighting: 'divided tongues, as it were of fire'. We might think of the whole of the rest of Acts of the Apostles as the continuation of this wind and fire.

The immediate effect is that 'they began to speak in different languages', and Luke allows us to overhear the comments of their astonished audience, who come from all over the known world. Despite the fact that the speakers are all Galileans, what they say is nevertheless understood by 'Parthians, Medes and Elamites' in the East, as well as (moving from East to West) 'inhabitants of Mesopotamia, Judea and Cappadocia, Pontus and Asia, Phrygia and Pamphylia'; then across the Mediterranean to Africa: 'inhabitants of Egypt and the parts of Libya around Cyrene', then to the North and East again: 'visiting Romans (both Jews and proselytes), Cretans and Arabs'. The message is delivered: 'we hear them speaking in

---

63. Or, possibly, 'for the same purpose'.

our own languages of God's great deeds'. Naturally not everyone is impressed, and some of the hearers mockingly accuse them of being 'full of sweet wine'. The Spirit leaves us free to decide whether or not to accept the message.

This little scene can serve as a dramatisation of the driving of the Spirit that will run through the whole of the rest of Acts. The tiny group of believers is now embarked on a journey from Jerusalem to Rome and to the ends of the earth (cf. 1:8). There will be many obstacles, including prison, death, and torture, as well as resistance and human sinfulness, but the Spirit's journey cannot in the end be thwarted. God remains both powerful and helpless.

A Lucan word: *poreuomai*

This can be very well illustrated by paying attention to two important Lucan words. The first is, in Greek, *poreuomai*, which means something like 'go', 'walk', 'journey', even at times with a hint of 'pilgrimage' about it. The point of mentioning it here is that it is the work of the Spirit. In classical Greek it can sometimes even mean to 'march'. The word appears many times in Luke, on its own or as a compound verb, and 44 times in Acts.[64] I will offer here just a few of the relevant texts.

In Acts 5:20, the angel of the Lord, having opened the gates, tells the imprisoned apostles, '*Go* and stand preaching in the Temple'. In 5:41 it is once more the apostles who, after being flogged and released, '*went off* rejoicing from the presence of the Sanhedrin, because they had been thought worthy of being dishonoured for the sake of the Name'. Then in 16:6, 7 we learn how the European mission started:

---

64. Though the translations inevitably do not always make this clear.

They came through Phrygia and the Galatian region, and were prevented[65] by the Holy Spirit from speaking the Word in Asia; then coming down by Mysia, they tried to *go* into Bithynia, and the Spirit of Jesus did not allow them.

And that is how they ended up in Troas, and went on to Macedonia, and how the highly successful mission to Philippi came about. All this 'journeying' is directed by the Spirit, sometimes by way of failure. In 18:6 Paul is rejected by the Jewish community and tells them, 'Your blood on your head; I am clean – from now on it is to the Gentiles that I am *going*'. We notice that this apparently simple word is part of Luke's rhetoric for indicating how the Spirit works in driving the mission.

The word is used again in 20:1, where it refers once more to the move from Asia (Ephesus in this case) to Europe (Macedonia): 'Paul summoned the disciples and bade them farewell and went out to *journey* into Macedonia'. On the way back, he has his famous encounter with the elders of Ephesus who have been summoned to Miletus to meet him, and among other things Paul tells them that he is 'bound by the Spirit to *journey* to Jerusalem, not knowing the things that are going to happen to me there' (20:22).

The next instance to mention is 22:5, 6, which is perhaps a bit odd since Paul is talking to a crowd in the Temple in Jerusalem about the journey to Damascus that he made, carrying letters from the High Priest and the Sanhedrin, when he encountered Jesus:

> I was *journeying* to Damascus, to bring the people (that is to say followers of Jesus) there in chains to Jerusalem for punishment. And it happened, as I *journeyed*, and drew near to Damascus . . .

---

65. *Kōluthentes*, another word of some importance in Acts.

However, Paul was presumably of the view, as he set off on that journey, that he was doing the Lord's work; as it turned out, the Lord had another journey in mind.

In 25:12 Paul is making his defence in the presence of Festus, the Roman procurator at Caesarea Maritima, and refuses to be sent back to Jerusalem for trial, as Festus had suggested. Instead, taking his stand on his Roman citizenship (see 22:25-9), Paul declares, 'I appeal to Caesar', to which Festus responds, after a hasty conference with his advisers, 'You have appealed to Caesar; to Caesar you shall *journey*.' Luke indicates by his choice of the word that the procurator is doing the Lord's work by enabling Paul's journey to Rome, where the story has been heading for so long.

Finally, let us look at the last two verses of Acts (28:30, 31). Paul is now safely in Rome, despite shipwreck and various attempts at murder, and even the attack of a poisonous snake. This is how the two-volume journey ends: '[Paul] remained for two whole years at his own expense, and gave hospitality to all those who *journeyed in* to him, preaching the kingdom of God, and the things about the Lord Jesus Christ . . .' We should observe a few things about this sentence.

- There is no reference to Paul's death. Now that he has reached Rome – 'the end of the earth' – his death (which the reader will certainly have known about) is irrelevant.
- 'Two whole years' is a very long time indeed in the context of Acts.
- The word that I have translated 'gave hospitality' is a very important idea in Luke's Gospel, and reveals that the Spirit is at work.
- We have the compound verb which I have translated, rather clumsily, as 'journeyed in'.

- There is a reference to the kingdom of God, which takes us back to Jesus' preaching of the gospel (Luke 4:43; 8:1), and to that of the disciples (9:2, 60).
- There is the reference to 'the things about the Lord Jesus Christ', which is, we have always to remind ourselves, what the Church exists in order to preach (and not itself).

So this ending to the 'Gospel of the Church' reminds us that it is on a journey which the Spirit directs, and which in consequence overcomes all obstacles. God may indeed be helpless, as we are insisting in this book, but God's project will be ultimately successful.

Another Lucan word: *akōlutōs*

I have cheated slightly in my translation, by leaving a gap (. . .) at the end of the passage quoted above. The missing words are of some importance, and let me start with the last word of the entire two volumes. That word is *akōlutōs*, and it means 'without being prevented'. The point here, at the very end of the two-Gospel journey, is that nothing at all can prevent the Spirit-led drive of the gospel. We saw the verb meaning 'prevented' a little earlier, referring to how in 16:7 the Spirit made sure that the gospel reached Europe. Nothing – neither opposition nor the sinfulness of Christians – can prevent the Spirit's journey and the preaching of the 'things about the Lord Jesus Christ'.

There is another phrase immediately before this, which I also omitted – namely 'with all confidence'. The Greek word that I have translated as 'confidence' is *parrhēsia*, which means something like the 'ability to say anything at all', and so 'boldness', or 'freedom', or (in a slightly different sense) 'liberty'. A possible translation is the Yiddish word 'chutzpah', which can mean 'cheek', in the sense of 'impertinence', or the freedom of the children of God. This is quite an important New Testament idea: we find it in Mark 8:32, where it describes the frankness with which Jesus was predicting his passion, and in John 7:26, where Jesus 'is speaking *openly*'. Compare 10:24, where his opponents demand that he tell them *openly* if he is the Messiah; 11:14 (Jesus talking about Lazarus having died); 16:25, where Jesus is telling his disciples 'openly' about the Father. The word also appears in significant contexts in Acts: 2:29, where Peter is pointing to the remarkable *boldness* of what he is saying. Compare 4:13, where it represents the Sanhedrin's perception of the *boldness* of Peter and John, despite their lack of education; and the prayer of the disciples for *boldness* in 4:29, and its effect in verse 31. Its appearance in 28:31 fits an existing pattern.[66] So this word is yet another sign that the Spirit represents the power of God underneath the apparent helplessness of the divine project.

John's Gospel's most original theological contribution: the Paraclete

The final section of this chapter on the Holy Spirit as God's response to the apparent helplessness of God's project is the word 'Paraclete', which is found only in John's Gospel and in the first Letter of John. Now this word is sometimes understood as 'Comforter', and it is true that the verb from which it comes can mean to 'comfort', and that idea certainly adds to our understanding of the term, but, for grammatical reasons with which I shall not bore you, it is probably best understood as a 'Defending Counsel' – one

---
66. And it is worth noticing that there are 16 further references elsewhere in the New Testament.

called to stand at our side. Interestingly, it does not refer only to the Holy Spirit, for Jesus is also a Paraclete.[66]

In the Gospel, there are just four sayings that use the word, and they are all from the Last Supper Discourse:

1. 14:16, 17, where the Paraclete's function is 'to be with you ... remain with you ... be amongst you'; and it[68] cannot be accepted, or seen, or known by 'the world'.
2. 14:26: here the function of the Paraclete is to 'teach and remind', and the Father sends it in Jesus' name.
3. 15:26, 27, where it is described as 'the Spirit of Truth, which comes out of the Father', and of it Jesus says that it 'will bear witness about me', and also enable the disciples to do the same.
4. Finally, in 16:7b-15 we have the longest, and in some ways the most obscure, of the four passages. In this one, the Paraclete is 'sent' to cross-examine the world on sin, righteousness and judgement, and its being sent is dependent on Jesus 'going away'. In addition to the cross-examination, the 'Spirit of Truth will guide you in all Truth', and 'will not speak on its own account, but will speak the things that it hears and announce to you'.

The Paraclete, then, is the 'Holy Spirit', and functions in the Last Supper Discourse as the answer to the 'sad question' that hangs over the little group, huddled together in the darkness: how can we survive without Jesus? The answer is, of course, that because of the Spirit, they do not have to: Jesus' absence means the presence of the Holy Spirit, from the Father, and sent by Jesus.

---

67. John 14:16; 1 John 2:1.
68. The word for 'spirit' is neuter in Greek, and it is quite hard to avoid the use of 'it', which has the added advantage of being inclusive language.

Conclusion

So the source of any authority in the Church is and can only be the Spirit.[69] The Spirit can never be forced or taken for granted, and therefore the authority it conveys must never be abused. That Spirit will guide us always on the journey, but those who aspire to leadership in the Church have to follow the Spirit's leading, not dictate where it goes, or what is to be taught.

Some questions for reflection

- What is the function of the Holy Spirit in the Church?
- Is there any connection between the Holy Spirit and what we have been calling the 'helplessness of God'?
- Does the Spirit point to a different way of exercising leadership or authority in the Church?

---

69. In this connection I am reminded of the true story of a well-known Archbishop and Cardinal, who when asked by evangelising Christians whether he had received the Holy Spirit, replied, 'We *give* the Holy Spirit.'

PART THREE
Leadership by listening

Introduction

So far in this book we have looked at the question of how authority is to be exercised in the Christian community, and we have seen how Pope Francis' method of governance may have been affected by his experience of the Spiritual Exercises of St Ignatius. To be honest, it does not much matter whether or not he has been affected in this way: not everyone undergoes the Exercises, and some kind of governing still has to take place in the Church. What matters is that this governing should be done with an eye on the only unrestricted authority – that of God.

We ended the previous chapter with the resurrection mood of Christians and the gift of the Spirit. What we are going to do now is to look at how that works out in the post-Easter life of the early Church. We shall do this by looking at two important documents of that period, namely, in the order in which they were written, Paul's first letter to the Corinthians, and Acts of the Apostles, which we have already been looking at under the heading of 'Resurrection'. We shall start with Acts, since we have already been reflecting upon it.

Acts is sometimes called 'The Gospel of the Holy Spirit', and I want to suggest that here (and in the life of the Church that it depicts) authority operates by listening, on the grounds that the Holy Spirit is at work, and therefore speaks to all Christians in a variety of ways. It follows, of course, that it is not merely the apostles who function as channels of the Spirit, but the people of God, individually and as a whole. The lesson for our time is evident. There are different kinds of listening in Acts – listening to the message of events, for example, and listening to fellow Christians – but none of them is any good unless they are also a listening to God.

There can be good listening and bad listening.

You may be asking at this stage what all this has to do with our title, 'The Helplessness of God'. It is simply that God is never-endingly nudging at our side, endeavouring to communicate, and we – that is to say we as individuals and we as Church – spend a good deal of time not listening, or in bad listening, hearing not God's gentle invitation but the seductions of our own selfish interests.

CHAPTER THIRTEEN

Listening in Acts

Listening to the Spirit: two important episodes

As we have seen, the start of it all in Acts is that first Pentecost, for which the reader has been long prepared (Acts 2:1-13).[70] Luke describes the effect in these terms: 'They were all filled with the Holy Spirit, and they began to speak in different languages, as the Spirit gave them to utter'.[71] The effect is ambiguous: some people assume that they must be drunk, while others 'are pierced to the heart' and demand to know 'what are we to do, brethren?' in the light of the accusation that they crucified Jesus. They are told that they have to 'repent and be baptised'. This they promptly do, and demonstrate a gift for listening, even to uncomfortable truths (verses 36-41).

Perhaps it might be best to look at two key episodes in Acts, where listening of various kinds takes place. They both concern what is arguably one of the deepest threads in Acts – that the gospel is going out to the Gentiles. The first is the episode of Simon Peter and the Roman centurion Cornelius in Acts 10. It starts with Cornelius listening to what the angel of the Lord tells him to do. We are told in verse 2 that he is a person of the right sort, so we are quite clear that he is going to make the correct response; indeed, the angel informs him that 'your prayers and acts of almsgiving have gone up for a remembrance offering in the presence of God'. We know therefore that God listens to him, and he to God,

---

70. See the command to wait for the 'promise of my Father' in Luke 24:49; cf. Acts 1:5, 8.
71. For possible meanings of 'different languages', and for some of the other difficulties in this passage, see Anthony C. Thiselton, *The Holy Spirit*, SPCK 2013, pp.51-57.

so we are not surprised when he does precisely what he is told (verse 8).

Next Luke paints the picture of Peter listening, explicitly in prayer, on the roof of his house. This time the picture is a bit more complicated, for Peter is hungry, and is instructed to 'eat' food that is unclean. Being a good Jewish boy, he refuses ('No way, Lord'), but he is instructed to listen to what God is doing (verse 15). This in turn leads him to meet and listen to the three emissaries from Cornelius, who has heard what the angel said to him.

We should notice that for both Peter and Cornelius there is discomfort at first with what they hear, but their attentive listening means that they will be used to advance God's project. Peter does what he is invited to do, assures Cornelius that his prayer has been 'heard'; and he is in turn listened to by the centurion and the Gentiles. He then utters a brief speech, offering an account of the Jesus story. Finally, Peter listens to the facts, when he realises that the Spirit has fallen on his audience,[72] and insists on their being baptised straightaway (verses 44-8).

More listening takes place in the next chapter, as the Christians in Jerusalem hear the news of this episode (verse 1),[73] which leads them first to criticise Peter. Then, having heard (verse 18), they are brought to an understanding of what God is doing: 'When they heard, they were quiet, and they glorified God.' This is a powerful episode, in which an outbreak of mutual listening leads those who were apparently opposed to each other to arrive at an unexpected conclusion that is clearly the will of God. The Church has been able to manage just such transformations at

---

72. With no account of what it means to have the Holy Spirit falling on them.
73. Significantly, 'they heard' is the very first word of the chapter.

several points in its history, and there seems to be an invitation now to some more listening.

The second episode, in Acts 15, is likewise a paradigm of the listening Church reaching a thoroughly revolutionary conclusion. It concerns the reaction of understandably conservative Christians from Judaea to a new departure that those in Antioch have launched – that of bringing non-Jews into the Jesus movement without insisting on their being circumcised (which is, after all, what the Bible demands). This provokes a crisis, the first of many in the long history of the Church that could have torn it apart.[74] Luke describes it as 'dissension and controversy' between the visitors from Jerusalem on the one hand, and Saul (never one to shirk controversy) and Barnabas on the other (verse 2). So the Christians in Antioch, instead of meekly bowing to the demands of the 'Mother Church', send 'Paul and Barnabas and some others of them to the apostles and elders in Jerusalem'. On the way to Jerusalem, they do some lobbying in Phoenicia and Samaria, causing 'much joy' among their fellow Christians. Lobbying is not, of course, entirely unknown in the contemporary Church.

When they reach Jerusalem, the debate starts: first, the delegation from Antioch 'announced what great things God had done with them'. Then the opposition has its say: 'Some of the party of the Pharisees who had come to faith arose, and said that it was necessary to circumcise them, and to tell them to keep the Law of Moses' (verses 4, 5).

After this we are witnesses to what sounds like a less public debate: a gathering of 'the apostles and the elders, to see about this matter'. As the temperature rises, Peter gets to his

---

74. We tend to forget that there have been dangerous crises in the Church in every era, and, wrongly, to think that our age is much worse than what has gone before.

feet and reminds them of the previous episode in chapters 10 and 11, how God chose him to preach to the Gentiles. He urges them 'not to tempt God, putting a yoke on the neck of disciples, such as neither we nor our ancestors had the strength to bear' (verses 7-11). What counts is faith, and the grace of the Lord Jesus Christ.

The next stage is an address by Barnabas and Paul, outlining 'what great signs and portents' God has worked through them (verse 12). Interestingly, we hear almost nothing of what they actually said, and nothing at all about the reaction they engendered. After this, in verses 13-21, it is the turn of James, the brother of the Lord, who seems to exercise a position of leadership in the Jerusalem Church. Rather surprisingly, he argues in favour of bringing Gentiles into the Church, and even finds an apt quotation from Amos to justify this revolutionary policy.[75] This opinion carries the day, and a letter is drawn up to give the result to the Christians in Antioch, and two delegates, one with an Aramaic and the other with a Greek name, are appointed to present the document. In the letter, the rigorists whose conservatism has caused anxiety in Antioch are roundly rebuked; it is stressed that the verdict is 'unanimous' (verse 25).[76] Christians are simply to avoid food offered to idols and which has not been properly slaughtered. They must also avoid sexual immorality. The verdict is then delivered to Antioch, where it is well received.

So the Holy Spirit helps them to find a radical new position that makes sense to those who have not been brought up in the Jewish traditions that had produced Jesus, Simon Peter and Paul. From this distance, it seems an

---

75. Amos 9:11, 12.
76. It is even agreed by the Holy Spirit – 15:28!

obvious verdict; without it the Church would simply not have survived. At the time, however, it was a daring – even shocking – innovation. They came to it, however, simply by listening – to each other, to the Law and, above all, to God, who speaks to us in many different ways.

Listening as obedience

Once you see it, this pattern of 'listening' (the Greek word can also mean 'hearing', and will not always come out obviously in translation) is everywhere you look. Let us now look at some more instances of this 'listening' in Acts. In chapter 3:12-26, Peter makes a speech to the 'people' (in Luke this always refers to faithful Israel), who are startled at the healing of a lame man in the Temple. He tells the story of Jesus, not omitting the standard accusation that his hearers had 'denied the Holy and Just One, and asked for a man who was a murderer to be given to you. You killed the Author of Life, whom God raised from the dead.' He even quotes Moses, arguing that the prophet had foreseen Jesus as God's Messiah and had told the people to 'listen to him with regard to everything that he says to you'.[77] The key is to learn to listen to Jesus.

That is the choice set before us in the next passage, Acts 4:13-22, where Peter and John have been dragged before the Sanhedrin. Here the official religious leaders have a problem, because they are startled at the 'chutzpah'[78] of these 'unlettered people', especially when they see the newly cured paralytic standing next to them. They cannot deny that a sign has taken place, so they try to forbid the two Galileans

---
77. Verse 22, citing Deuteronomy 18:15, 16.
78. The Greek word used here is *parrhēsia* which, as discussed in the previous chapter, means 'the ability to say anything at all', and is often translated as outspokenness, frankness, fearlessness.

to say anything or to teach in the name of Jesus. The reply of Peter and John is to ask 'if it is right in God's presence to listen to you rather than to God'. This 'listening' is key here, for all religious authorities, and the primary focus of our attention must be listening to God. As Peter and John say, 'We cannot not speak of the things that we have seen and heard'. Their courageous stance is vindicated by the infilling of the Holy Spirit, 'and they started speaking God's word with chutzpah' (Acts 4:31).

'Listening' is not very far removed from 'obeying' (that is what the word means in Hebrew, Greek and Latin). In 5:17-42 the religious authorities arrest them again, and they are released from gaol by 'an angel of the Lord', who tells them to preach in the Temple. Peter simply insists that 'it is necessary to obey God rather than human beings'. Not surprisingly, this evokes immense fury among their hearers, who 'want to kill them', so there is such a thing as bad listening. However, the religious authorities listen to one of their own number – Rabban Gamaliel – and restrict themselves to flogging the apostles and instructing them (improbably enough) 'not to speak in the name of Jesus'. The disciples' response is what you might have predicted, and is evidently the right kind of deafness: 'they did not rest from teaching and gospelling that Jesus is Messiah'.

'Obedience' or 'listening' is the heart of the matter; you might contrast the 'great crowd of priests' who 'obeyed the faith' in 6:7 with the refusal to obey with which Stephen charges 'your ancestors' in the story that immediately follows (7:39). Stephen invites them to 'listen' at the beginning of his speech, and their response at the end (verse 54) – 'when they heard they were cut to the quick, and ground their teeth at him' – is a standard establishment reaction which clearly bodes ill. It contrasts with what God does: 'I have heard their groaning' (7:34, quoting Exodus 3:7).

The Church needs to listen also to events, which can be the speech of the Holy Spirit to us, rather than thinking that nothing can ever change. This is what the 'apostles in Jerusalem' did when 'they heard that Samaria had heard the word of God' (8:14). Their response is to send Peter and John, who have, of course, already proved themselves to be good listeners. They lay hands on the Samaritan Christians, which brings the Holy Spirit down upon them. In the same chapter, Philip does the same for the puzzled Ethiopian eunuch when he 'heard him reading Isaiah the prophet', and so started a conversation that culminated in the baptism of the eunuch and the disappearance of Philip (8:26-40).

Listening to Jesus

The next episode in 9:1-30 recounts Paul's encounter with Jesus, which likewise involves a good deal of attentive 'hearing' or 'listening'. First of all Saul hears a voice, as he falls to the ground in response to a sudden light from heaven. And the voice seems to know a good deal about him, addressing him by name, 'Saoul, Saoul', and asking, 'Why are you persecuting me?' It then emerges that in persecuting Jesus' followers Saul is persecuting Jesus, and that what the Jesus movement has been saying is after all true – that God raised him from the dead, and that it is appropriate to use of him the language that those Christians have been employing. 'Lord,' he says, using the divine title without realising what he is uttering.

Paul is not the only one who has to listen, for Ananias is told something quite unexpected – that Saul of Tarsus is in a particular house, and that Ananias has to go and lay hands on him so that he recovers his sight. Ananias, however, knows better:

> Lord – I have heard [that word again] from many people what great evils he has done in Jerusalem on the saints; and here he has authority from the High Priests, to tie up all those who call upon your name.
>
> *Acts 9:13, 14*

Nevertheless he has to do what he is told, with the remarkable result that Saul turns up in the synagogues: 'he was preaching Jesus, that this one is the Son of God' (verse 20).

This in turn leads to another kind of hearing:

Listening to Paul

> All those who heard him were amazed, and started saying, 'Isn't this the one who in Jerusalem was ravaging those who called upon this name, and has come here for the very purpose of leading them in chains to the high priests?'
>
> *Acts 9:21*

Once again, intelligent and godly listening leads to very unexpected results, and we must expect church leadership to get to grips with this sort of attentive hearing.

When Paul comes to preach the first sermon of his new apostolic career, it is at Antioch in Pisidia, in the synagogue in that culturally mixed city. Initially it is highly successful, and the listening is very attentive. 'As they went out, [the people] begged that this message should be spoken to them on the following Sabbath (13:42). This brings immense crowds, and the opponents 'were filled with jealousy and spoke out against the things uttered by Paul, using insults' (verse 45). The upshot is ambiguous: 'the Gentiles were delighted when they heard, and they glorified the word of the Lord', while their opponents 'stirred up the leading women who were believers, and the leading people of the city, and they aroused a persecution against Paul and Barnabas and flung them out of their territory' (verses 48-50). Different kinds of hearing go on here. This may suggest a useful criterion for our listening: good listening does not arouse hatred.

The next bit of listening comes in chapter 16, and it is what brings the gospel to Europe for the first time. The geography is slightly unclear, but we are told that:

> [Saul and Barnabas] were prevented by the Holy Spirit from speaking the word of God [in the Roman Province of] Asia. And when they came to Mysia, they tried to journey to Bithynia, and the Spirit of Jesus did not allow them.[79]
>
> *Acts 16:6, 7*

We are not told how this is done, but presumably it involves the apostles listening. They end up in Troas – an excellent port for access to Northern Greece or 'Macedonia' – and there they are obliged to do some more listening:

> a vision appeared to Paul at night. A certain Macedonian man was standing and begging him and saying, 'Come across to Macedonia and help us'. When he saw the vision, immediately we sought to go out to Macedonia, concluding that God had summoned us to preach the gospel to them.
>
> *Acts 16:9, 10*

This was a highly successful piece of listening, with effects that are with us today, including the widely held illusion that Christianity is a European phenomenon.

This brings them to Philippi, which was to be an important centre for the Macedonian mission, and to the wealthy and significant church leader, the redoubtable Lydia.

---

79. Bithynia and Mysia are in North-West Asia Minor.

We learn that this 'Purple-seller from the city of Thyatira, a God-worshipper, was listening; and the Lord opened her heart to pay attention to the words uttered by Paul' (16:14). Her listening is the prelude to her conversion, and this leads her to make a request, which in turn gains a listening:

> When she had been baptised, she and her household, she begged [us], saying, 'If you have decided that I am faithful to the Lord, come into my house and stay there.' And she forced us.
> *Acts 16:15*

The listening is mutual, it seems, and a model for what we should be doing within Christianity today. Nor is that the only hearing that takes place in Philippi, for there is a slave-girl with a 'Python' spirit, who hears Paul and identifies him and Silas as 'slaves of the Most High God, who are proclaiming a way of salvation to you'. She is quite right, of course, but Paul becomes annoyed and exorcises her, which means that she is no longer of any use to her owners (16:16-19). So she is heard in a rather different way.

This all leads to the imprisonment of Paul and Silas, and in turn to another sort of listening on the part of their gaoler (16:23-40). He has been instructed to make sure that these two criminals do not escape. They spend the night 'praying and singing hymns to God'. Significantly, perhaps, 'the prisoners were listening to them'. The upshot is 'a great earthquake, so that the foundations of the prison were shaken and all the gates were immediately opened, and all the chains were loosened'. The gaoler assumes that they have all escaped and is about to commit suicide when Paul stops him, and he listens, as does his entire household: 'they spoke the word of the Lord to him, along with all those in his household'. After this piece of listening he washes their wounds, takes them home and feeds them and (apparently out of embarrassment) the city counsellors want to set them free. Paul instead makes them come to the prison and let them out in person. This is a different kind of listening.

There is more listening to come. In Thessalonica and Berea Paul speaks and at first is heard sympathetically, but then agitators who do not want to listen cause ructions (17:2-9, 10-13). Then in Athens, Paul delivers a speech at the Areopagus, carefully crafted with quotations from the Greek poets. They listen attentively enough until he starts to talk about resurrection – the heart of his gospel. At that point they roar with laughter, or tell him to come back later. Just a few, however, have heard the message (17:16-34).

In Acts 18:1-11 Paul is in Corinth, which might not at first sight appear to be a likely place for people to listen. It was enormously wealthy, notorious for sexual immorality, and had pronounced economic and social disparities. There, however, Paul found a hearing, notably with a husband-and-wife team[80] of Roman Jews who, like Paul, were tent-makers. Although there was, once more, a good deal of opposition, 'many of the Corinthians who listened came to faith, and were baptised'. And Paul himself has to listen, once more, for

> The Lord told Paul at night, through a vision, 'Don't be afraid; instead speak, and don't be silent. For I am with you and no one will attack you and do you harm, because I have a great number of people in this city.' He stayed a year and six months, teaching God's word among them.
> *Acts 18:9-11*

Not everyone in Corinth is uniformly good at listening, however, as we shall see when we look at Paul's first letter to that fractious church. And one of those who is not especially good at listening is Apollos from Alexandria, who turns up

---

80. Priscilla and Aquila.

in Ephesus (18:24-8). He is described as 'eloquent . . . catechised in the Way of the Lord, and burning in the spirit, he was speaking and talking accurately the things about Jesus; he only knew John's baptism'. Priscilla and Aquila, friends of Paul, as we have already seen, 'took him in hand and expounded God's Way to him more accurately'. So his eloquence only takes him so far, and we may reflect on the fact that in Alexandria, where he comes from, they have quite a lively and attractive way of reading the Scriptures. We may also notice that 'he wanted to go through Achaea' of which the capital is precisely Corinth, which Paul has just left. It may be that Apollos is not switched to listening mode but is doing simply what he wants, even though 'his fellow-Christians encouraged him, and even though he powerfully refuted the Jews, and demonstrated that Jesus is the Messiah'. Later on, as we shall see, there is tension between Paul and Apollos, and it may simply be that he does not listen enough.

Others in that early Church have not 'heard' enough, including some disciples whom Paul meets in Ephesus who have 'not even heard that a Holy Spirit exists'. Once they have 'heard' this, they are 'baptised into the name of the Lord Jesus'. Then Paul laid hands on them, 'the Holy Spirit came upon them, and they started speaking in tongues and prophesying' (19:2, 5, 6). That is good listening.

What is perhaps a less impressive instance of listening is the story of Paul's speech on his farewell visit to Troas, which left no space for hearing, or for noticing that he was sending some of his audience to sleep:

> On the first day of the week, when we had gathered to break bread, Paul was lecturing them, because he was going to depart on the next day; and he extended his lecture until

midnight! Now there were a good many lamps in the upper room where we had gathered, And a young man called Eutychus was sitting on the window-sill, and was borne down by a deep sleep, as Paul lectured on and on, and he was carried down by sleep, and fell down from the third floor, and was taken up dead! Paul went down and fell upon him, and embraced him and said, 'Don't be disturbed. For his life is in him. He went up and broke bread, and tasted a bit and conversed until dawn. And so he departed. They took the boy up alive, and were comforted in no small measure.

Acts 20:7-12

It seems that Paul has not learnt a thing, but has fallen into the religious leader's habit of talking and not listening. Or is that unfair?

There is an interesting, and perhaps somewhat ambiguous, example of listening a little later on, when Paul and his companions, on their way back to Jerusalem, have reached Caesarea and the house of Philip and his four prophetess daughters (21:8-14).[81] Into this maelstrom comes Agabus, a prophet from Judaea, who predicts that 'in Jerusalem the Jews will tie up [Paul] and hand him over to the Gentiles'. Luke tells us that 'when we heard this, we and the locals begged him not to go up to Jerusalem'. Paul takes no notice at all, and Luke records their reaction: 'when Paul did not give in, we shut up, and said, "May the Lord's will be done."' We are left asking who has been listening most attentively here. Agabus is correct, of course, as the rest of the narrative makes clear. Is Paul wrong to pay no attention? And are Paul's companions correct in pushing the matter no further? Certainly it is our task to listen to what the Lord is saying in the here and now, but it may not always be clear which of

---

81. One feels that it must have been a somewhat noisy household.

several possibilities – each advanced by good people – is in fact what the Lord is asking of us.

When Paul reaches Jerusalem, Luke tells us about what might have been a rather tense meeting between Paul, who was not over-inclined to put up with other people's authority, and James and all the elders (21:17-27). Paul takes the initiative and recounts 'in detail what God had done among the Gentiles through [Paul's] ministry'. With some relief we hear that they have been listening, for they 'heard and glorified God'. Then, however, they raise another matter, to which it will be important for Paul to listen, namely that he is walking into a hornets' nest because there are Jews alleging that he is against the Law and customs of Moses. So they suggest a piece of spin doctoring – for Paul to demonstrate that he is an observant Jew (which was not precisely accurate). Paul hears them and goes along with their suggestion, but to no real avail, since 'some Jews from Asia' organise a riot against him, and he is arrested.

Listening and not listening to Paul

Listening and refusing to listen continue in 22:1-22. Paul narrates to his co-religionists in the Temple the story of his encounter with Jesus, and all that has happened since then. His Jewish audience listens to him, until the moment when he quotes Jesus as saying to him, 'Go. For I am sending you far away to the Gentiles.' At that point things become decidedly ugly, and this is deemed to be sufficient grounds to kill him. Listening is not the name of the game.

We watch the unfolding of the story as it rushes to its end (bar a two-year delay in prison in Caesarea Maritima). Paul is arraigned before Festus, who has succeeded the previous procurator, Felix. He eventually tells Herod Agrippa, who is visiting with his wife Bernice, what he has discovered: he has been listening well, it seems, since he has grasped that the issue concerns 'some queries about their own superstition that they have against him. And about someone called Jesus, a dead man whom Paul alleges is alive' (25:19). Festus has certainly got that right; he has heard *something*.

Then Paul makes his speech to Agrippa, and there is a good deal about listening here (26:2-23). First, he says to Agrippa, 'I ask you to hear me with patience.' Secondly, he cites what he himself has heard: 'I heard a voice saying to me in the Aramaic language, "Saoul, Saoul, why you do persecute me?" And the Lord said, "I am Jesus, whom you are persecuting."' as a result of which Paul is made 'a minister and witness of what you have seen, and what I am going to show you'. That is the kind of listening that we expect to find among leaders in the Church.

Finally, then, we come to the last piece of listening that Acts presents to us. In chapter 28, the story finally arrives in Rome, where it has been heading these many chapters, and there Paul gathers the leading Jews of the city (verses 17-31). They deny having 'heard' anything to his discredit, and simply say, 'We think it appropriate to hear from you what you think.' When the appointed day comes, some of them 'were persuaded, but others did not believe'. Paul takes this as insufficient listening and says, 'Let it be known to you that this salvation of God has been sent to the Gentiles – *they* will listen.'

This great work now ends with the gospel being freely proclaimed, as Paul was 'preaching the kingdom of God and teaching the things about the Lord Jesus Christ with all freedom,[82] without being prevented'. Paul has finished his listening, and there are others who are ready to listen. The

---

82. Our old friend 'chutzpah/parrhēsia'.

Acts of the Apostles is a powerful story, and we shall do well to learn from it about how to 'hear' in our day.

Gazing at the picture-gallery: listening to the Spirit

Luke is a gifted artist, and it is no accident that scenes from his two-volume work have attracted the brush of painters down the centuries. One of the ways he expresses the gospel is by drawing pictures and inviting us to contemplate them, and so to listen to what the Spirit is saying to us. He does this by means of what are sometimes called Luke's 'summaries'.

What happens if you really listen to what the Spirit says? These generalised pictures give us an idea of what Luke thought the early Church looked like when it was functioning properly and listening to its Lord. Luke means us to reflect on them in order to see where we might learn to listen, and so respond to the helplessness of God. They are a model for the Church in any age, as it strives to pay attention to God.

The first of these pictures is to be found in Acts 1:13, 14, in the aftermath of Jesus' ascension. They are obedient to the command he gave them in Luke 24:49, and simply remain in the upper room, 'persisting unanimously in prayer, with women, and with Mary the mother of Jesus, and with his brothers'. So the first time we see the early Church, everyone is present, and they are all praying. That is what makes possible the events that follow; and we are called to imitate this attentive prayerfulness in our day.

The second 'Lucan summary' is in 2:42-7, after the events of Pentecost. It describes the effect that this 'listening Church' had on its contemporaries:

> They were persevering in the teaching of the apostles and in fellowship, in the breaking of the bread and in prayers. There came awe upon every soul, and many portents and signs took

place through the apostles. All the believers were on the same mission; and they had everything in common. They would sell their possessions and property, and divide them according as anyone had need. Each day they persevered unanimously in the Temple, breaking bread at home. They shared food in joy and simplicity of heart, praising God, and having favour with all the people. And the Lord added each day those who were being saved, on the same mission.

Our tendency is to look gloomily at passages of this sort and to mutter, 'That was then; this is now.' In fact, it was no easier for them than it is for us, and there has never been a time when the Church was without its divisions. We are, however, invited to work for the qualities that are outlined here: 'persevering in the teaching of the apostles' (that is to say, primarily, the resurrection of Jesus); 'fellowship', which is an excellent test of the reality of our Christian living; praying together; and breaking bread together. In addition, there is awe on those who observe them, as is the case with those who look at the witness that is being given today by Pope Francis. Then there is their generosity to the poor, their loyalty to the Temple[83] and to the Eucharist and shared meals, and their attentiveness to God. Not surprisingly, this attracted the attention of 'the people'[84] and drew new believers. There is something for us to contemplate here, as we learn once more to listen.

The next 'Lucan summary' is at 4:31-5, and a similar picture is painted with Luke's characteristically broad brush:

they were all filled with the Holy Spirit, and they were speaking God's message with chutzpah. The crowd of believers had a single heart and a single soul; not one of them

---
83. The old story of God, where Luke's Gospel began and ended: Luke 1:9 and 24:53.
84. For Luke this is always the Jewish people.

said that their possessions were their own – they had everything in common. With immense energy the apostles used to give their witness to the Lord Jesus' resurrection, and there was great grace on all of them. No one among them was in need; for anyone who owned lands or houses sold them, and they brought the price of what they sold, and put them at the feet of the apostles, and it was distributed to each of them, according as each had need.

Once again we see the effect of attentive listening: the Holy Spirit comes upon them and they are enabled to be free about preaching the gospel, especially the central message of the resurrection. Not only that, but we encounter the first known instance of communism, where no one had possessions of their own but it was to each in accordance with their necessity, from each according to their needs. If you find yourself becoming depressed at how much better those early Christians were than we, their successors, then read the episode of Ananias and Sapphira (Acts 5:1-11), which is hardly ever read in church, and recognise that not much has, after all, changed, and there is still an obligation on us not to 'lie to God', or 'test the Lord's Spirit'.

Another of Luke's summaries immediately follows that disedifying little episode:

> Through the agency of the apostles, many signs and portents took place among the people; and they were, all of them, of one mind in Solomon's portico. None of the others dared to join with them, but the people were loud in their praise. And a great many more believers were added to the Lord, crowds of men and women, with the result that they brought the sick out into the public squares and put them on beds and stretchers, for Peter's shadow to fall on them when he came.
>
> *Acts 5:12-15*

Again we are given a similar picture of an impact on the people, a public demonstration of what they were doing, and widespread attraction for the populace at large. This is what can happen when we once more learn to listen attentively.

The summaries become shorter now; they have perhaps done their work. The next one appears in the following chapter:

> The word of God increased and the number of disciples in Jerusalem multiplied very greatly; and a great crowd of priests were obedient to the faith.
> *Acts 6:7*

There are many erudite guesses about the identity of the 'great crowd of priests' who are 'obedient' or 'listening' to the faith. The point is the transformation effected by their attentiveness to God.

The next summary is just after the newly converted Saul arrives in Jerusalem, and then has to be smuggled out to Caesarea and thence to his native city of Tarsus:

> The Church had peace throughout the whole of Judaea and Galilee and Samaria, being built up, and advancing in fear of the Lord, and was filled with the comfort of the Holy Spirit.
> *Acts 9:31*

The point here seems to be that they are all looking out for each other, even protecting the far-from-easy figure of Paul. Interestingly, their spread mirrors the journey that Jesus had made in the Gospel – Galilee, Samaria, Judea, Jerusalem – and now we can see the spread of the mission that was given to them in Acts 1:8. This is what happens when the Church listens to God.

The attentiveness continues throughout; another summary tells us what it was like in Antioch:

THE HELPLESSNESS OF GOD

> There were in Antioch, through the church that was there, prophets and teachers: Barnabas and Symeon called Niger, and Lucius of Cyrene, and Menahem who had grown up with Herod the tetrarch, and Saul. As they served the Lord and fasted, the Holy Spirit said to them, 'Set apart for me Barnabas and Saul, for the work that I have summoned them to.'
>
> *Acts 13:1, 2*

The message, you see, is spreading across the world. It speaks to people of different languages and cultures, for the names are Aramaic and Hebrew and Greek and Latin, and at least one of them is from Africa. They are all, however, listening to the Spirit, and that marks the start of the mission of Paul which will dominate the rest of Acts. Once again, we are invited to contemplate what happens when we listen to God.

There are just two more summaries, which may be allowed to speak for themselves. The first is set in Ephesus, just before Paul starts his final journey back to Jerusalem: 'So, through the power of the Lord, the word grew and strengthened' (19:20). It speaks of the Lord's power, but we should notice that the episode that immediately precedes it is that of the exorcists who realised that there was money and fame to be had and tried to hijack the name of Jesus, with nearly catastrophic results. God's power is not to be abused.

The final Lucan summary we have already mentioned; it is the last verse of the whole two-volume story that is Luke–Acts, and it tells us that Paul 'was preaching the kingdom of God, and teaching the things about the Lord Jesus Christ, with all chutzpah, without being prevented' (28:31). We have now reached Rome, the 'ends of the earth' foreshadowed in Acts 1:8, and the very last phrase (a single word in Greek) indicates that nothing can stop the spread of the gospel. It shares in the self-effacing power of God —but human beings have to listen.

Some questions for reflection
- Is leadership by listening a possible model for us today?
- To whom are we called to listen?
- What makes listening difficult?

CHAPTER FOURTEEN

An exercise in mutual listening?
1 Corinthians

Paul's correspondence with those fractious Corinthians can speak to us today, as we learn the art of listening. Paul is endeavouring to exercise authority over them, but they are not unduly impressed. Of course, he has to listen to them too (and to others), and it seems to be the case that when we fail to listen to each other, God is (to return to the title of our book) quite helpless.

There are several kinds of listening in this letter: what Paul has heard; then what you might call 'the Apollos problem'; there is the Corinthian insistence on 'word' or 'rhetoric', which they thought was worth listening to; there is the helplessness of Paul, which means that he has to depend on God; there is also the question of Paul's forgetfulness, which may have come across as a way of not listening; then there are the Corinthian slogans to which Paul has to listen. Finally he brings them to the heart of the message, and the importance above all of listening to Christ. That will be the secret for us today, as we learn about listening in the Church, as our way of responding to God's helplessness.

Listening: what Paul has heard

The first thing that we notice is that Paul has heard from 'Chloe's people' (1 Corinthians 1:11) that 'there are quarrels among you' – apparently concerning personality cults surrounding Paul, Apollos and Kephas (and, as Paul adds, perhaps with dark humour, 'Christ'). He has also heard that there are divisions[85] at the Eucharist (11:18), and that there is sexual immorality of an extreme kind in the church in Corinth. So the first kind of listening is a matter of knowing what is going on.

The Apollos problem

We discover as we listen that Paul has heard that there is a problem of some kind, a tension between Apollos and Paul. It comes up, lightly camouflaged, in the very first chapter. When he expands on what he has heard from 'Chloe's people', he says, 'Each of you is saying: "I'm a Paul man"; "I'm an Apollos man"; "I'm a Kephas man".' Then Paul ends with a grim little joke of his own, when he says, 'Well – I'm a Christ man!' (1:12).

The tension seems to centre on the figures of the apostles who converted them. It may be that Apollos, though he knew less than Paul, had a more engaging style of explaining the Scriptures as part of his spreading the message of Christ. Kephas is something of an irrelevance here; he only appears a few times more,[86] and I suspect that he is used in the letter only as a distraction from the real tension between Paul and Apollos. So from 3:4–4:21 Paul indulges in a long section in which he and Apollos are described in terms of two metaphors, one from gardening (3:6-8), and the other from architecture (3:9-17). This also enables him to play for the first time with the idea of the 'holy Temple of God' (3:17), which will be a useful image for talking about the unity that a building requires (for example, 8:1), and which the church in Corinth conspicuously lacks. It sounds as though the power struggles

---

85. He uses the Greek word *schismata*, which, significantly perhaps, has 50% of all its New Testament appearances in 1 Corinthians.
86. 3:22; 9:5; 15:5.

that have been all too frequent in the history of the Church were operative in Corinth, and the Corinthians (and perhaps also Apollos) needed to be reminded that apostles are 'servants and stewards' (4:1).

It seems that Paul may be in a delicate position, not able to let go at Apollos with both barrels, as is sometimes his tendency. The final mention of him comes in 16:12, just as he is finishing the letter. It may be that some people have accused Paul of preventing Apollos from coming to Corinth, for here he writes:

> Regarding brother Apollos, I begged him many times over that he should come to you with the brothers and sisters; and it was not at all the will that he should come. But he will come when the time is ripe.
> *Acts 16:12*

What is 'the will'? Some scholars think of it as 'God's will', but it is perhaps easier to understand it as 'Apollos' will', and a statement that, given the current embarrassment, it is Apollos, and not Paul, who is responsible for the former's continued absence from Corinth. It is impossible for us at this range to be sure, but one thing we can see is that Paul is listening to both Apollos and the fractious Corinthians, and so trying to find a way out. This is a handy model for leadership in the Church.

Some words for refusing to listen

There are three words in 1 Corinthians that seem to have been keywords in the Corinthian church, no doubt thrown at Paul to show that he is not up to much (possibly by contrast with Apollos). The words are (in Greek) *logos*, *sophia* and *gnosis*. As many people will probably know, they are standardly translated as 'word', 'wisdom' and 'knowledge', but it may help to capture the problem that Paul sees with them if instead we use the terms 'rhetoric', 'cleverness' and 'so-called knowledge'. The precise translation does not matter; the point is that Paul regards these three terms as naming a profound threat in Corinth. They are qualities that the Corinthians are demanding, and to which they give a high rating, but which, in Paul's estimation, represents on their part a refusal to listen.

We can look now at some of the texts in which these important words appear. *Logos* comes at the very beginning, in 1:5, where it is joined by *gnosis*: '. . . because you have been enriched in all respects in him, in all *logos* and all *gnosis*'. Here the point is that the 'enriching' is not something that they have done, but something that God has done to them. So they cannot claim any credit for it (though the Corinthians may not realise this until they have got a bit further into the letter).

In 1:17 it appears again, this time in conjunction with *sophia*: 'Christ did not send me to baptise but to preach the gospel, and not in cleverness of rhetoric, so that the cross of Christ should not be emptied out'. The point here, presumably, is that Christ's cross is the very epitome of his 'helplessness', and in demanding *logos* and *sophia* and *gnosis* the Corinthians are refusing to deal with Christ's helplessness; they want something a good deal more educated and powerful.

In the next verse, Paul does something very daring indeed, for he starts a series of contrasts between the way God looks at things and the way human beings (especially the arrogant characters in Corinth) look at things. Our tendency is to demand *logos* and power but instead God offers us 'folly' and 'weakness'. Read slowly through verses 18-25 and see how extraordinary is the contrast. It comes to its climax with these thoroughly shocking lines: 'The stupid bit of God is wiser that human beings; and the weak bit of God is stronger than human beings.' Our biblical worldview (and Paul has grasped this with his accustomed clarity) turns the world's outlook quite upside down.

Next read the opening verses of the next chapter.[87] Here Paul is reminding the Corinthians of his helpless state when he arrived in Corinth,[88] and the technique that he adopted for preaching the gospel:

> I came to you, brothers and sisters, not with any superior rhetoric or superior cleverness, when I announced God's mystery to you. I had decided, you see, not to know anything among you, apart from Jesus Christ – and him crucified! I arrived with you in great fear and trembling, and my rhetoric and my preaching was not a matter of persuasive clever rhetoric, but of the demonstration of the Spirit and energy. I did not want your faith to be a matter of human cleverness; I wanted it to be a matter of God's energy.[89] We do talk of cleverness among initiates, but not the cleverness of this world, or the rulers of this world. Instead we talk of the cleverness of God, mysterious and hidden, which God marked out ahead of time before the ages, for our glory. None of the rulers of this world had *gnosis* of this cleverness; if they had done, they would never have crucified the Lord of Glory.
>
> *Acts 2:1-8*

It is hard to imagine a better way of describing God's powerful helplessness. Paul continues the contrast a few lines later: 'the things that we are uttering are not a matter of the

---
87. The reader will do well to have an alternative translation open while reading my version.
88. From Athens, after a clever speech had been received with roars of derisive laughter, according to Acts 17:32–18:1.
89. 'Power', strictly speaking.

taught rhetoric of human cleverness, but of what the Spirit has taught us' (2:13).[90]

Another word that Paul uses frequently in 1 Corinthians, always to describe those who are opposed to him, can be translated as 'puff up', or its passive participle, 'those who are puffed up'. It refers to the insubstantial nature of those who are becoming arrogant with all their *logos* and *gnosis* and *sophia*. This word appears for the first time in 4:18:

> Some people have got puffed up, on the grounds that I was not coming to you. I'm going to come to you soon enough (if the Lord wills), and then I shall know for certain, not just the rhetoric of Those-Who-Are-Puffed-Up, but their power. You see, God's kingdom is not a matter of rhetoric, but of [real] power.[91]

Sometimes Paul can use these terms in a way that is a little less aggressive. For example, when he is trying to sort out the divisions caused by their abuse of the gifts of the Spirit, and listing those gifts in terms of their contribution to building up the body, he says, 'Some people, through the Spirit, are given a rhetoric of cleverness,[92] others a rhetoric of *gnosis*, in accordance with the same Spirit' (12:8).

You get the picture, and we do not need here to speak at length about *gnosis* and *sophia*. Paul uses *gnosis* in chapter 8, where he is starting to address the tricky question of whether it is permissible to eat food that has been offered to idols. This, whether by buying such food in the meat market or by accepting an invitation from a pagan friend to dine with them in their temple, represented a fairly cheap way of

---

90. Once again the reader will do well to compare this translation with other renderings.
91. Then, just to show that Paul himself is not above a bit of power-politics, he threatens them with corporal punishment (4:21)!
92. Or 'a word of wisdom'.

obtaining protein. The problem here was that if a fellow Christian were to see you eating such a meal, they might misinterpret it as implying that you had gone over to the pagan gods. It looks as though some of the Corinthians have been constructing an argument on the basis that 'we all have knowledge', and that therefore we know that pagan 'gods' are not gods at all. Paul accepts their claim that 'we have *gnosis*', but reminds them of another, higher consideration – that of love, and comments, 'love builds up. If someone thinks that they have *gnosis*, they do not have it in the way they should have it. But if someone loves God, that person is known by God' (verses 1-3). *Gnosis*, that is to say, is a two-way street: there were people in Corinth claiming to have it; but God also has *gnosis*, and they need to pay attention to that, and to defend their 'weaker brethren' (cf. verses 9-12). Leadership in the Jesus movement is absolutely bound to pay attention to the weak.

It follows therefore that these potentially admirable qualities of *logos*, *sophia* and *gnosis* are not the only questions to be considered. In chapter 12 Paul puts all three words into the same sentence (verse 8), but only as part of a much larger list of qualities given to the body of Christ, which the Spirit is meant to build up. *Gnosis*, he never tires of stressing, is irrelevant (cf. 13:2, 8; 14:6).

Paul does the same, as we have already partly seen in 1:17-24, with *sophia*. It is not an absolute requirement, but a useful weapon in the evangelist's armoury.[93] And what looks like power to the 'chattering classes', who were so dominant in Corinth, is in fact entirely inadequate: 'The cleverness of this world is idiocy in God's presence', he reminds them (3:19); human beings have to learn to embrace God's helplessness.

---

93. 1:17-30; cf. 2:6-7, where the idea appears three times.

Does Paul listen?

You may be wondering at this point whether Paul does any of the listening that this book claims is intimately involved in leadership in the Jesus movement. We have seen him laying about him with some gusto – and we have only been looking at one of his letters! Certainly he seems well aware of his limitations; we have already seen, for example, his helplessness when he first arrived at Corinth (2:1). And he coyly admits to his forgetfulness when he first denies having baptised any of the Corinthians, then is reminded of Crispus and Gaius, and, finally is nudged to recall 'the household of Stephanas', which leads him to a less dogmatic statement: 'apart from that, I'm not sure if I baptised anyone else' (1:14-16).

Certainly Paul evidently listens to his audience. In 9:1-5 he makes that very clear, starting with a series of indignant rhetorical questions:

> Am I not free? Am I not an apostle? Didn't I see Jesus our Lord? Are you not my work in the Lord? Even if I am not an apostle to others, I am at least to you; for you people are the seal of my apostolate in the Lord. This is my defence to those who put me on trial: don't we have permission to eat and drink? Don't we have permission to take a Christian wife around with us, as do the rest of the apostles, and the brothers of the Lord, and Kephas?

Clearly he has been listening to them, even if he is not wholeheartedly in agreement with those who oppose him.

Do the Corinthians listen?

One of the problems that evidently beset the Corinthians was their deafness. This comes out in the chaos of their liturgy (14:26-33a), and they have to be reminded that 'God is not a God of confusion but of peace', because they have been doing what they like, regardless of anyone else, with a 'psalm, a teaching, a revelation, a tongue, an interpretation'. They have not learnt to listen, and they need to be taught. One of the dangers of having spiritual experience is that because it is so overwhelming, you think that you know it all, and that 'those other people' don't really matter.

Likewise, it looks as though some of the women at Corinth may have been calling out to each other, or possibly to their husbands, to find out what has just been said (verses 33b-6)[94] Certainly the Corinthians in general are not particularly respectful of one another; it seems from the closing verses that they have been looking down at 'the household of Stephanas' (whom Paul had apparently baptised; cf. 1:16), instead of looking up to them, as Paul wishes (16:15-18). We cannot claim to be Christian unless we take all our fellow members of the body of Christ absolutely seriously.

What is more, as we have already seen, it seems that the Corinthians may have been indulging in sloganeering, which is an excellent way of refusing to listen to one another.[95] As we have already seen, one of their slogans is 'I can do what I like' (6:12), which may have been their reinterpretation of Paul's gospel of freedom, which has to be reinterpreted in terms of whether or not it 'builds up' (10:23). Another slogan is apparently 'it is good for a man not to touch a woman' (7:1);[96] another is, as we have seen, 'we all have knowledge' (8:1). Slogans are the refuge of lazy thinkers.

---

94. If this was indeed in the original letter (not all the manuscripts agree).
95. Compare, perhaps, the way in which today words like 'conservative' or 'liberal' are used as a way of not having to listen to the people so labelled.
96. This may have been the slogan of an ascetic party in Corinth who thought Paul was sympathetic to that point of view. Paul's approach is rather more reflective.

What is the heart of Paul's gospel?

This brings us neatly back to the question that this book is considering: how should we exercise authority or power in the Jesus movement? To answer this we have first to decide what the Jesus movement is for. Paul gives his answer, and we should pay careful attention to it. It is noticeable today that when people are asked to define the central beliefs of Catholicism, they come up with all sorts of different answers. This is Paul's view:[97]

> I'm reminding you, brothers and sisters, of the gospel that I gospelled you, which you received, on which you take your stand, through which you are being saved, in what terms I gospelled you, as long as you hold to it (unless you believed in vain). For I passed down to you in the first place, what I had also received, that Christ *died* for our sins, in accordance with the scriptures, and that *he was buried*, and that *he was raised* on the third day according to the scriptures, and that *he appeared* . . .
>
> *1 Corinthians 15:1-5*

This, as we have seen, is sometimes referred to as the 'gospel of four verbs', emphasising the reality of Jesus' death and the certainty that God raised him from the dead. That is the primitive gospel, and we shall not do well to make anything else the centre of our proclamation, especially not if the other material gives us an excuse for beating fellow Christians over the head and denouncing them as being less than orthodox.

The opening verses of the letter give a different take on this. The Corinthians, as we have seen, were rather inclined to congratulate themselves on their own spiritual achievements; when people go in for self-congratulation, bullying can lie

---

[97]. We have already looked at this text from another angle, but it is worth repeating under this heading.

not very far behind. So when Paul starts this reply to a previous letter, he uses a series of 'passive' adjectives to emphasise how they have had it all done for them and have not achieved it by themselves. The 'passive' adjectives[98] are printed in italics:

> Paul *called* as an apostle of Christ Jesus through the will of God, and Sosthenes the fellow-Christian, to the church of God which is in Corinth, to *those who have been made holy* in Christ Jesus, *called to be saints*, along with all those who call upon the name of our Lord Jesus Christ in every place, theirs and ours. Grace and peace to you from God our Father and the Lord Jesus Christ. I give thanks to my God all the time about you with regard to the grace *which has been given you* in Christ Jesus, because in every respect *you have been enriched* in him, in all rhetoric and all gnosis, just as the witness of Christ *has been strengthened* in you. So that you lack no *gift*, as you wait for the *revelation* of our Lord Jesus Christ. *He will confirm* you to the end as irreproachable on the day of our Lord Jesus Christ. God is faithful, through whom *you have been called* into the fellowship of his son Jesus Christ our Lord.
>
> *1 Corinthians 1:1-9*

The point is fairly clear, though the Corinthians may not have tumbled to it as it was first read out to them. All their spiritual qualities are not their own doing, but the gift of God, and they have nothing on which to pride themselves. It follows from this that any exercise of authority in their church, or indeed in any of our churches, needs to be done with a degree of humility. And Paul applies this even to himself, since he starts off by emphasising that he is on the same footing as they are, since he too is '*called*'.

---

98. In two cases a noun, and in one case the active verb 'he will confirm' makes the same point.

There is another lesson here, moreover. You may have noticed that the words 'Christ' and 'Jesus' are used no less than 17 times in that passage. That is the clue, not only to understanding Paul but also to handling the difficult question of authority in the Church. Faith is not a matter of getting everyone to sign up to a set of propositions; it is a matter of keeping our eyes on Jesus, and that means gazing where Jesus gazed, unshakably on God.

That is how Paul solves his problems: on divorce 'not I, but the Lord' gives the answer to the difficult question (7:10; cf. 11:23, on the Last Supper); on the related question about those who are not (yet) married (7:12; cf. verse 25), it is Paul, 'not the Lord'. It is important for church authorities to make this distinction fairly carefully. Paul, however, is quite prepared to invoke the Lord's authority in the case of those who think that they are 'a prophet or a spiritual person': 'let them recognise that it is a command of the Lord' (14:37).

Finally, and by way of conclusion to this brief book, let us recall the words of Paul in his final (and alas unsuccessful) attempt in this letter to persuade the Corinthian Christians to stop fighting and bullying one another. This is how authority is to be exercised in the Church, and we should be imperceptive not to notice that the picture of love is in fact a portrait of Paul's beloved Jesus. This is the way ahead for authority in the Church:

> And I am showing you a still more excellent way:
> If I speak the languages of human beings and of angels,
> but I do not have love – I have become an echoing bronze, or
> a tinkling cymbal.
> And if I have prophecy and I know all mysteries and all knowledge,
> and if I have all faith, so as to move mountains, but I do not have love

– I am nothing.
And if I dole out all my possessions
and if I hand over my body in order to boast, but I do not have love
– I am not helped.
Love is patient, love is kindly, it is not jealous, it does not bear a grudge;
it does not show off, is not puffed up, does not behave dishonourably,
does not seek its own, does not get roused to anger, does not count up evil,
does not rejoice over injustice, but rejoices along with the Truth.
Love bears everything, believes everything, hopes everything, endures everything.
Love never fails:
As for prophecies, they will be cancelled out. Tongues? They shall cease.
Knowledge? It will be cancelled out.
For we know in part and we prophesy in part; but when the perfect comes,
what is partial will be cancelled out.
When I was an infant, I used to talk like an infant; I used to think like an infant; I used to count like an infant.
But when I became an adult, I cancelled out infant things.
For at present we see in a mirror, in a riddle; but then it will be face to face.
At present I know in part; but then I shall know, just as I am known.
So now there remain these three things: faith, hope, love.
And the greatest of these is love.
1 Corinthians 12:31b–13:13

There is nothing more to be said.

AFTERWORD

Discernment

What can we say at the end of this brief investigation of the biblical models of leadership? What have we learnt from applying them to the shape of the Spiritual Exercises of Ignatius Loyola, which have so radically affected the inner journey of our present Pope Francis?

One thing that seems clear is that authority in the Church is not to be exercised from the top downwards. It is instead, after the manner of those Spiritual Exercises, to be a question of discerning what God is saying to us, listening to each other, searching for what the Spirit is saying to the Church.[99] Now we have to be careful here, for it is all too easy to fool ourselves into thinking that we have heard the voice of God when in fact all that we have heard is the projection of our own selfishness. However, Ignatius Loyola is well aware of this difficulty, and puts before the retreatant some admirably common-sense 'Rules for the Discernment of Spirits' (Exercises 313-336).[100] The way ahead seems to lie in dialogue or conversation, and in taking the biblical narratives seriously precisely as open-ended story.

---

99. See Revelation 2:7, etc.
100. See Munitiz and Endean, *Saint Ignatius Loyola: Personal Writings*, pp.348-353.

www.ingramcontent.com/pod-product-compliance
Lightning Source LLC
Chambersburg PA
CBHW020410080526
44584CB00014B/1265